The Giant Book of True Facts

by
Jake Jacobs

* * * * *

Published by Jake Jacobs

1.

Sutter's Fort, located in present-day Sacramento, California, is a historic landmark that played a significant role in the early history of California.

2.

The fort was built in 1839 by John Sutter, a Swiss immigrant and pioneer who established the first non-Native American settlement in the Sacramento Valley.

3.

Sutter's Fort served as a trading post, agricultural center, and base of operations for Sutter's enterprises, including farming, ranching, and trade.

4.

The fort was constructed using adobe bricks made from clay and straw, with walls measuring 2.5 feet thick and standing at a height of 18 feet.

5.

The fort enclosed an area of approximately 1.75 acres, featuring a central courtyard surrounded by various rooms and buildings.

6.

Sutter's Fort was designed as a self-sufficient establishment, with facilities such as a blacksmith shop, bakery, distillery, carpenter's shop, and more.

7.

The fort included residential quarters for Sutter and his family, as well as housing for employees and visitors.

8.

Sutter's Fort served as a refuge and trading hub for European and American immigrants traveling to California during the 1840s.

9.

The fort became a significant center of commerce, attracting trappers, traders, Native Americans, and other individuals seeking goods and services.

10.

Sutter's Fort was strategically positioned along the California Trail, a major overland route used by pioneers heading to the American West.

11.

The fort's location made it an important stop for travelers, providing a place to rest, resupply, and repair wagons before continuing their journey.

12.

During the California Gold Rush in 1848, Sutter's Fort played a central role as the discovery of gold in the nearby American River brought thousands of prospectors to the region.

13.

The influx of gold seekers resulted in a significant transformation of the fort and its surroundings, as it became a bustling center for gold-related activities.

14.

Sutter's Fort became a temporary seat of government for the California territory in 1849, hosting the Constitutional Convention that drafted California's first state constitution.

15.

The fort's central location and influence led to the establishment of the city of Sacramento, which grew around the fort's original site.

16.

Sutter's Fort was a focal point for early agriculture in California, with Sutter introducing various crops, including wheat, corn, grapes, and vegetables, to the region.

17.

The fort's agricultural operations included orchards, vineyards, and livestock raising, making it a vital source of food for settlers and travelers.

18.

The fort's blacksmith shop was instrumental in providing essential services, such as repairing wagons, horseshoeing, and fabricating tools and equipment.

19.

Sutter's Fort was an important center for cultural exchange, with Native Americans, Europeans, and Americans interacting and exchanging goods and ideas.

20.

The fort's trade connections extended to the Pacific coast, with goods transported to and from ships at the port of Yerba Buena (later renamed San Francisco).

21.

Sutter's Fort served as a base for several expeditions exploring and mapping the interior of California, including the famed Fremont Expeditions.

22.

The fort's location made it vulnerable to attacks during times of conflict. In 1846, during the Mexican-American War, the fort was briefly captured by a group of American settlers known as the Bear Flaggers.

23.

After the discovery of gold, the fort's importance waned as Sutter's lands were overrun by gold seekers, leading to financial difficulties for Sutter.

24.

Following Sutter's financial setbacks, ownership of the fort changed hands multiple times, and it eventually fell into disrepair.

25.

In 1890, the Native Sons of the Golden West, a historical organization, purchased Sutter's Fort and began restoration efforts to preserve its historical significance.

26.

The fort was designated a California Historical Landmark in 1931 and was added to the National Register of Historic Places in 1966.

27.

Today, Sutter's Fort State Historic Park encompasses the original fort's site and features reconstructed buildings and exhibits that depict life during the early years of California's history.

28.

The central building within the fort is the two-story adobe central building, which served as Sutter's residence and administrative center.

29.

The central building contains a museum that showcases artifacts and exhibits related to the history of the fort and the California Gold Rush era.

30.

Visitors to Sutter's Fort can explore the various rooms and buildings, including the blacksmith shop, bakery, and carpenter's shop, to gain insights into the daily activities of the fort's inhabitants.

31.

The fort's interior courtyard is a peaceful space where visitors can relax and enjoy the atmosphere, surrounded by the adobe walls and historical structures.

32.

Sutter's Fort hosts special events and demonstrations, such as blacksmithing and candle making, to provide visitors with a hands-on experience of life in the 19th century.

33.

The fort's location in the heart of Sacramento allows visitors to explore the vibrant city and learn about its rich history and cultural heritage.

34.

Sutter's Fort has been featured in various films and television shows, including "California Gold Rush" and "Gold Rush."

35.

The fort's historical significance extends beyond California, as it represents the pioneering spirit and the impact of westward expansion in the United States.

36.

Sutter's Fort has become an educational destination, offering school programs and guided tours that provide students with an immersive experience of California's history.

37.

The fort's architecture showcases the adobe construction techniques prevalent in the region during the 19th century, reflecting the cultural influences of the time.

38.

The fort's preservation and restoration efforts have involved extensive research to ensure historical accuracy in the reconstruction of the buildings and the interpretation of the site.

39.

Sutter's Fort serves as a reminder of the challenges faced by early settlers in California, the clash of cultures, and the transformative impact of the California Gold Rush.

40.

The fort's museum exhibits a diverse collection of artifacts, including tools, furniture, clothing, and personal items, providing a glimpse into the daily lives of the fort's inhabitants.

41.

Sutter's Fort has become a popular destination for history enthusiasts, offering a unique opportunity to step back in time and experience the frontier spirit of early California.

42.

The fort's location near the American River provides visitors with the chance to explore the natural beauty of the surrounding area, including hiking trails and recreational activities.

43.

Sutter's Fort has inspired numerous artistic works, including paintings, photographs, and literary pieces that capture its historical significance and architectural beauty.

44.

The fort's restoration efforts have involved collaboration between historical preservation experts, architects, and archaeologists to ensure the site's authenticity.

45.

Sutter's Fort has been a focal point for historical research, contributing to our understanding of early California history and the challenges faced by pioneers during westward expansion.

46.

The fort's influence extends beyond its physical boundaries, with its historical significance recognized through educational programs, publications, and academic studies.

47.

Sutter's Fort serves as a gathering place for cultural events, such as reenactments, festivals, and celebrations that commemorate California's early history.

48.

The fort's visitor center provides information about the site's history, offers interpretive exhibits, and features a gift shop where visitors can purchase souvenirs and educational materials.

49.

Sutter's Fort has become an iconic symbol of Sacramento's heritage and a must-visit destination for tourists and locals interested in exploring the state's early history.

50.

The fort's enduring legacy lies in its ability to transport visitors back in time, allowing them to connect with the pioneers, Native Americans, and diverse individuals who shaped California's rich and dynamic history.

51.

The Swedenborgian Church, also known as the Church of the New Jerusalem, is a Christian denomination that follows the teachings of Emanuel Swedenborg, an 18th-century Swedish scientist, philosopher, and theologian.

52.

The church was founded in the United States in 1787 by a group of individuals who were inspired by Swedenborg's spiritual writings.

53.

Emanuel Swedenborg's works, such as "Heaven and Hell" and "Divine Love and Wisdom," form the foundation of the Swedenborgian Church's beliefs and practices.

54.

The Swedenborgian Church emphasizes the belief in the spiritual unity of all religions and encourages dialogue and cooperation among different faith traditions.

55.

The church holds that Swedenborg had a spiritual awakening and received revelations from God, which he recorded in his extensive writings.

56.

Swedenborg's teachings focus on the concepts of inner spiritual transformation, the afterlife, and the interconnectedness of the spiritual and physical realms.

57.

The Swedenborgian Church places a strong emphasis on the importance of personal spiritual growth and the pursuit of a loving and ethical life.

58.

The church recognizes the Bible as a sacred text but interprets it in the light of Swedenborg's teachings, seeking spiritual and symbolic meanings beyond the literal sense.

59.

Swedenborgians believe in the existence of a spiritual world that is intricately connected to the physical world and that spiritual growth continues after death.

60.

The Swedenborgian Church embraces a non-dogmatic approach, encouraging individuals to explore and interpret Swedenborg's writings in a personal and meaningful way.

61.

The church values reason, science, and intellectual inquiry, believing that faith and rationality can coexist harmoniously.

62.

Swedenborgian worship services often incorporate a blend of traditional Christian elements, such as prayers, hymns, and scripture readings, with reflections on Swedenborg's teachings.

63.

The Swedenborgian Church promotes inclusivity and welcomes individuals from all walks of life, regardless of their race, gender, sexual orientation, or religious background.

64.

The church believes in the essential goodness of all people and the importance of cultivating compassion, kindness, and love towards others.

65.

The Swedenborgian Church has a strong tradition of social activism and community involvement, advocating for social justice, environmental stewardship, and humanitarian causes.

66.

The church places a special emphasis on the idea of spiritual marriage, which is the union of love and wisdom within an individual's character.

67.

Swedenborgian worship spaces, known as "churches of the New Jerusalem," often feature unique architectural designs that reflect a blend of traditional and modern influences.

68.

The Swedenborgian Church has a decentralized structure, with individual congregations having a considerable degree of autonomy in their practices and governance.

69.

The church has an ordained ministry, with pastors serving as spiritual leaders, teachers, and facilitators of worship and community activities.

70.

Swedenborgian rituals, such as baptism and marriage ceremonies, focus on the inner spiritual significance of these sacraments rather than their external symbolism.

71.

The Swedenborgian Church values the exploration of dreams and visions as potential avenues for spiritual insight and guidance.

72.

The church recognizes the importance of both individual spiritual experiences and communal worship in nurturing spiritual growth.

73.

Swedenborgians believe in the existence of angels and spirits who play a role in guiding and supporting individuals on their spiritual journey.

74.

The Swedenborgian Church has a long history of engaging in interfaith dialogue and cooperation, seeking common ground with other religious traditions.

75.

Swedenborgian hymns and music often emphasize themes of love, peace, and spiritual harmony, with a focus on inner contemplation and meditation.

76.

The church's teachings emphasize the concept of "usefulness," encouraging individuals to find meaning and purpose in their daily lives by serving others and contributing to the betterment of society.

77.

The Swedenborgian Church celebrates a number of annual festivals and holy days, including Easter, Christmas, and Pentecost, with services and rituals that reflect its unique theological perspectives.

78.

The church recognizes the importance of spiritual community and provides opportunities for fellowship, support, and shared exploration of Swedenborg's teachings.

79.

Swedenborgian theology includes the belief in divine providence, the idea that God's guidance and care are present in every aspect of life.

80.

The Swedenborgian Church has had a significant impact on literature, art, and philosophy, influencing prominent figures such as Ralph Waldo Emerson, William Blake, and Henry James.

81.

The church has a tradition of encouraging spiritual seekers to engage in personal study and reflection on Swedenborg's writings, inviting individuals to form their own understanding of the teachings.

82.

Swedenborgians place a strong emphasis on the power of love and charity, believing that genuine faith is expressed through acts of kindness and compassion towards others.

83.

The Swedenborgian Church affirms the inherent dignity and worth of every human being, valuing the diversity of human experiences and perspectives.

84.

The church recognizes the importance of prayer as a means of connecting with the divine and seeking spiritual guidance and support.

85.

Swedenborgian theology includes the concept of "conjugial love," which refers to the spiritual union between a husband and wife that extends beyond the physical realm.

86.

The Swedenborgian Church has an international presence, with congregations and affiliated organizations in various countries around the world.

87.

Swedenborgian publications, such as The New Church Messenger and The New Philosophy, provide forums for sharing ideas, insights, and reflections on Swedenborgian teachings.

88.

The Swedenborgian Church supports education and intellectual exploration, sponsoring study groups, lectures, and seminars on topics related to spirituality, theology, and philosophy.

89.

The church places a strong emphasis on the cultivation of virtues such as humility, honesty, patience, and forgiveness as integral aspects of spiritual growth.

90.

Swedenborgians believe in the concept of spiritual regeneration, the ongoing process of inner transformation and growth towards greater alignment with divine love and wisdom.

91.

The Swedenborgian Church recognizes the importance of the natural world and encourages environmental stewardship and sustainable living practices.

92.

Swedenborgian theology emphasizes the idea that true religion is not confined to external rituals and beliefs but is expressed through a genuine commitment to living a life of love and service.

93.

The church encourages individuals to seek spiritual insights from a variety of sources, including nature, the arts, and scientific discoveries, recognizing the interconnectedness of all aspects of creation.

94.

Swedenborgian worship often incorporates periods of silence and contemplation, allowing individuals to connect with their inner selves and the divine presence.

95.

The Swedenborgian Church maintains a rich tradition of sacred music, with hymns and compositions that reflect the spiritual themes and values of the faith.

96.

Swedenborgians believe in the importance of spiritual freedom and the individual's ability to make choices in accordance with their understanding of truth and goodness.

97.

The church has a tradition of spiritual healing and offers support to individuals seeking physical, emotional, and spiritual well-being.

98.

Swedenborgian theology includes the concept of spiritual correspondence, the idea that the natural world reflects spiritual realities and truths.

99.

The Swedenborgian Church values intellectual honesty and encourages open-minded exploration and questioning of spiritual concepts and beliefs.

100.

Swedenborgians are engaged in ongoing efforts to apply the principles of Swedenborgian theology to contemporary issues, seeking to promote justice, peace, and spiritual renewal in the world.

101.

The Galapagos Land Iguana (Conolophus subcristatus) is a species of lizard endemic to the Galapagos Islands.

102.

It is one of three species of land iguanas found in the Galapagos, the other two being the Conolophus pallidus and Conolophus marthae.

103.

Galapagos Land Iguanas are large reptiles, with males reaching lengths of up to 3 feet (1 meter) and weighing around 25 pounds (11 kilograms).

104.

They have a distinct appearance with rough, bumpy skin and a unique coloration that ranges from yellowish-brown to grayish-black.

105.

The Galapagos Land Iguana has a long, spiny crest along its back and neck, which distinguishes it from other iguana species.

106.

These iguanas are primarily herbivorous, feeding on leaves, fruits, and the pads of prickly pear cacti.

107.

Galapagos Land Iguanas have a specialized digestive system that allows them to process and extract nutrients from the tough vegetation they consume.

108.

They have an extremely slow metabolic rate, which allows them to survive on a low-calorie diet and go for long periods without eating.

109.

Galapagos Land Iguanas are well adapted to the arid environment of the Galapagos Islands and can tolerate high temperatures and limited water sources.

110.

They have a unique nasal gland system that helps them expel excess salt from their bodies, allowing them to drink seawater when fresh water is scarce.

111.

Land iguanas play an important role in seed dispersal, as they consume fruits and then excrete the seeds elsewhere, aiding in the distribution of plant species.

112.

They are also known to dig burrows in the ground, which provide shelter and protection from extreme temperatures and predators.

113.

Galapagos Land Iguanas have a lifespan of up to 50 years, making them one of the longest-lived reptiles in the world.

114.

These iguanas are social animals and can often be found in large groups known as colonies or aggregations.

115.

During the breeding season, male Galapagos Land Iguanas become territorial and engage in aggressive displays to establish dominance.

116.

Males develop bright yellow or orange coloration on their skin during the breeding season to attract females.

117.

The females lay their eggs in shallow burrows or depressions in the ground and cover them with soil for protection.

118.

After an incubation period of around 90 days, the hatchlings emerge from the eggs and are fully independent from birth.

119.

The main predators of Galapagos Land Iguanas are introduced species such as feral cats and dogs, which prey on the young and eggs.

120.

They are also susceptible to diseases introduced by non-native species, highlighting the vulnerability of the Galapagos Land Iguana population.

121.

Galapagos Land Iguanas have played a crucial role in the study of evolution, as Charles Darwin studied them during his famous voyage on the HMS Beagle.

122.

The population of Galapagos Land Iguanas faced significant decline in the past due to habitat destruction and predation by introduced species.

123.

Conservation efforts, including the eradication of invasive species and habitat restoration, have helped in the recovery of the Galapagos Land Iguana population.

124.

The Galapagos Land Iguana is listed as vulnerable on the IUCN Red List of Threatened Species, highlighting the need for ongoing conservation measures.

125.

The species is protected under Ecuadorian law, and the Galapagos National Park authorities closely monitor and manage their populations.

126.

Galapagos Land Iguanas are an iconic symbol of the Galapagos Islands and are a popular attraction for tourists visiting the archipelago.

127.

The distinct features and unique adaptations of the Galapagos Land Iguana have made it an important subject of scientific research and study.

128.

The Galapagos Land Iguana has played a significant role in shaping the biodiversity and ecology of the Galapagos Islands through its interactions with the environment and other species.

129.

Galapagos Land Iguanas have been observed engaging in a behavior known as "basking," where they sunbathe to raise their body temperature and aid digestion.

130.

These iguanas have an excellent sense of smell, which they use to locate food sources and identify potential predators.

131.

The Galapagos Land Iguana has a relatively small population size compared to other iguana species, primarily due to its restricted range and historical threats.

132.

Climate change poses a significant threat to the Galapagos Land Iguana, as rising temperatures and changing weather patterns can affect their food sources and habitat.

133.

The Galapagos Land Iguana is a flagship species for conservation in the Galapagos Islands, representing the unique wildlife and fragile ecosystems of the archipelago.

134.

The Charles Darwin Research Station in the Galapagos Islands conducts research and conservation efforts focused on the Galapagos Land Iguana and other endemic species.

135.

Efforts are underway to restore and protect the natural habitats of the Galapagos Land Iguana, including the removal of invasive plant species and reforestation projects.

136.

The Galapagos Land Iguana is an important indicator species for monitoring the overall health and balance of the Galapagos Island ecosystems.

137.

The conservation success of the Galapagos Land Iguana can serve as a model for the protection and management of other endemic species in the Galapagos Islands.

138.

Galapagos Land Iguanas are known for their docile and calm temperament, allowing researchers and tourists to observe them closely without causing disturbance.

139.

The Galapagos Land Iguana has inspired artists, photographers, and filmmakers who have captured its unique appearance and behavior in various forms of media.

140.

Due to their iconic status, Galapagos Land Iguanas are often featured in educational materials and documentaries about the Galapagos Islands and its wildlife.

141.

Galapagos Land Iguanas have unique adaptations to survive in harsh environments, including their ability to withstand long periods without food or water.

142.

The presence of Galapagos Land Iguanas is an important ecological indicator, as their abundance or decline can reflect changes in the ecosystem's health.

143.

The Galapagos Land Iguana's distinct appearance and evolutionary adaptations have made it an important example of convergent evolution and natural selection.

144.

Galapagos Land Iguanas are not known to swim, as their short, sturdy limbs are not well-suited for aquatic locomotion.

145.

The conservation of Galapagos Land Iguanas requires ongoing efforts to protect their habitats and manage the impacts of human activity in the Galapagos Islands.

146.

The Galapagos Land Iguana has become an emblematic species for Galapagos National Park, representing the unique wildlife and ecological significance of the islands.

147.

The Galapagos Land Iguana's ability to survive in harsh conditions and consume tough vegetation demonstrates the remarkable adaptability of life in extreme environments.

148.

The Galapagos Land Iguana is an important tourist attraction, with visitors from around the world coming to observe and learn about this unique reptile species.

149.

The Galapagos Land Iguana is a key component of the Galapagos Islands' tourism industry, contributing to the local economy through eco-tourism and supporting conservation efforts.

150.

The Galapagos Land Iguana serves as a symbol of the Galapagos Islands' ecological importance and the need for sustainable practices to protect its fragile ecosystems for future generations.

151.

The Galapagos Lava Gull (Leucophaeus fuliginosus) is a unique and rare bird species endemic to the Galapagos Islands.

152.

It is the rarest gull species in the world, with an estimated population of fewer than 400 individuals.

153.

The Galapagos Lava Gull is predominantly found on the coasts and rocky shorelines of the Galapagos Islands, particularly on the islands of Santiago, Isabela, and Fernandina.

154.

These gulls have a distinctive appearance, with a large, white body, dark gray or black wings, and a yellow or reddish-orange bill.

155.

Juvenile Galapagos Lava Gulls have a different plumage, with mottled brown and white feathers, which gradually molt into the adult plumage over several years.

156.

Galapagos Lava Gulls are opportunistic feeders and have a varied diet that includes fish, squid, crustaceans, and scavenged carrion.

157.

They are known for their feeding behavior of following fishing boats and scavenging from the discarded fish or offal.

158.

The Galapagos Lava Gull is a seabird that is well adapted to its marine habitat, with webbed feet and strong wings for efficient flight and foraging over the ocean.

159.

They have excellent maneuverability and can perform graceful aerial displays, soaring and diving near the water's surface.

160.

The Galapagos Lava Gull is a monogamous bird, and pairs form long-term bonds, often returning to the same nesting sites year after year.

161.

These gulls typically breed in colonies on rocky cliffs or islets, making nests from twigs, grass, and other available materials.

162.

The breeding season of the Galapagos Lava Gull occurs between October and December, with females laying one to three eggs in a clutch.

163.

The incubation period lasts about 28 days, with both parents taking turns incubating the eggs.

164.

Galapagos Lava Gulls display cooperative breeding behavior, with non-breeding individuals assisting in defending the nesting territory and caring for the young.

165.

The chicks hatch with fluffy down feathers and are cared for by both parents, who provide food and protection.

166.

Galapagos Lava Gull chicks grow quickly and are capable of flight and independence within a few months.

167.

The Galapagos Lava Gull is known for its calm and gentle nature, often allowing humans to approach relatively close without displaying aggressive behavior.

168.

They have a low reproductive rate, with only one successful breeding attempt per year, which contributes to their vulnerability and slow population growth.

169.

Galapagos Lava Gulls face various threats, including habitat disturbance, pollution, introduced predators, and disturbance from human activities.

170.

Conservation efforts are underway to protect and monitor the Galapagos Lava Gull population, including habitat restoration and controlling introduced species.

171.

The International Union for Conservation of Nature (IUCN) classifies the Galapagos Lava Gull as endangered, emphasizing the need for immediate conservation actions.

172.

The unique adaptations and limited distribution of the Galapagos Lava Gull make it an important indicator species for monitoring the health of the Galapagos marine ecosystem.

173.

The Galapagos Lava Gull is considered an "island endemic" species, as it is found exclusively within the Galapagos Islands and nowhere else in the world.

174.

Galapagos Lava Gulls have been observed engaging in kleptoparasitism, stealing food from other seabirds such as Blue-footed Boobies and Frigatebirds.

175.

These gulls have a lifespan of up to30 years in the wild, although accurate data on their longevity is limited.

176.

The Galapagos Lava Gull has been recognized as a flagship species for the conservation of the Galapagos Islands' unique and fragile ecosystem.

177.

They play an important role in nutrient cycling and maintaining the ecological balance of the marine and coastal environments they inhabit.

178.

The Galapagos Lava Gull is protected under the laws of Ecuador, with specific regulations in place to safeguard their habitat and populations.

179.

The gulls are highly adapted to the harsh environmental conditions of the Galapagos Islands, including extreme temperatures and limited freshwater resources.

180.

The Galapagos Lava Gull's large, dark wings provide effective camouflage against the volcanic landscapes of the islands.

181.

They have a keen sense of vision, enabling them to spot potential food sources in the water or on the shores.

182.

The Galapagos Lava Gull's coloration serves as a form of disruptive camouflage, helping them blend in with the rocky coastal environment and avoid predation.

183.

Their scavenging behavior plays an important ecological role in cleaning up carrion and preventing the spread of disease in their environment.

184.

The Galapagos Lava Gull's population decline is primarily attributed to habitat destruction and the introduction of non-native predators, such as rats and cats.

185.

Climate change and its impact on sea levels and oceanic conditions may pose additional threats to the Galapagos Lava Gull's nesting sites and foraging habitats.

186.

The Galapagos Lava Gull's decline in population has led to its inclusion in various conservation programs and initiatives aimed at protecting the Galapagos Islands' unique biodiversity.

187.

Researchers and conservationists continue to study the Galapagos Lava Gull to better understand its ecological role, behavior, and specific conservation needs.

188.

The Galapagos Lava Gull is an important part of the Galapagos Islands' natural heritage and serves as a symbol of the delicate balance between human activities and the preservation of unique wildlife.

189.

Their presence and conservation status highlight the need for sustainable tourism practices and responsible behavior in fragile ecosystems like the Galapagos Islands.

190.

Galapagos Lava Gulls are sensitive to disturbance, and human activities such as habitat destruction and pollution can disrupt their natural behaviors and reproductive success.

191.

The Galapagos Lava Gull's diet includes both marine and terrestrial sources, allowing them to adapt to changing environmental conditions and food availability.

192.

The Galapagos Lava Gull's nesting sites often overlap with those of other seabird species, leading to competition for resources and potential interactions.

193.

Galapagos Lava Gulls are known for their unique vocalizations, producing a variety of calls and sounds to communicate with one another.

194.

The decline in the Galapagos Lava Gull population has prompted collaborative conservation efforts between government agencies, non-profit organizations, and local communities.

195.

The Galapagos Lava Gull's breeding success is influenced by the availability of food resources and the stability of nesting sites.

196.

They are known to engage in territorial displays, including calling, wing-flapping, and aggressive posturing, to defend their nesting areas.

197.

Galapagos Lava Gulls are often observed roosting in large groups on offshore rocks and islets, providing protection from predators and communal warmth.

198.

The Galapagos Lava Gull's large beak and sharp talons are well-adapted for capturing and consuming a variety of prey items.

199.

The decline in the Galapagos Lava Gull population is a concern not only for their species but also as an indicator of the overall health of the marine ecosystem they depend on.

200.

TheGalapagos Lava Gull's survival is intricately tied to the conservation of the Galapagos Islands as a whole, emphasizing the importance of protecting their habitats and implementing sustainable practices to ensure their long-term viability.

201.

Verizon Communications, commonly known as Verizon, is an American multinational telecommunications conglomerate that was founded on June 30, 2000.

202.

The company's roots trace back to the Bell Telephone Company, which was founded by Alexander Graham Bell in 1877.

203.

Verizon was formed as a result of the merger between Bell Atlantic Corporation and GTE Corporation.

204.

The merger between Bell Atlantic and GTE was one of the largest mergers in corporate history, creating a telecommunications giant with a market capitalization of over $100 billion at the time.

205.

Verizon's name is a combination of the Latin word "veritas" (meaning truth) and the word "horizon," representing the company's commitment to providing reliable and trustworthy communication services.

206.

Verizon is headquartered in New York City and has grown to become one of the largest telecommunications companies in the world.

207.

The company operates in multiple sectors of the telecommunications industry, including wireless communications, broadband, and landline services.

208.

Verizon's wireless network is one of the largest and most advanced in the United States, providing coverage to millions of customers across the country.

209.

In addition to its wireless services, Verizon also offers high-speed internet and digital TV services through its FiOS brand.

210.

Verizon has played a significant role in the development and deployment of 5G technology, which promises faster internet speeds and enhanced connectivity.

211.

The company has invested billions of dollars in building and expanding its 5G network infrastructure to meet the increasing demands of connected devices and emerging technologies.

212.

Verizon has a long history of acquisitions and partnerships, allowing it to expand its services and reach new markets.

213.

In 2015, Verizon acquired AOL, a leading internet media company, to strengthen its digital content and advertising capabilities.

214.

In 2017, Verizon acquired Yahoo, another prominent internet company, and merged it with AOL to form Oath Inc., which was later rebranded as Verizon Media.

215.

Verizon has a strong focus on corporate social responsibility and has implemented various sustainability initiatives to reduce its environmental impact.

216.

The company has made significant investments in renewable energy sources and aims to achieve carbon neutrality in its operations.

217.

Verizon has a robust philanthropic program, supporting various educational and community-based initiatives, particularly in the areas of STEM education and domestic violence prevention.

218.

The company has been recognized for its commitment to diversity and inclusion, with initiatives aimed at promoting equal opportunities for employees and fostering an inclusive work environment.

219.

Verizon has a history of supporting disaster relief efforts, providing communication services and resources during times of crisis.

220.

The company played a crucial role in the aftermath of the September 11, 2001 attacks, restoring communication services in affected areas and supporting emergency responders.

221.

Verizon was an early adopter of unlimited data plans, offering customers the freedom to use data without worrying about overages.

222.

The company has been at the forefront of innovation, introducing various technologies and services to enhance the customer experience.

223.

Verizon was one of the first telecommunications companies to launch a nationwide 4G LTE network, providing faster internet speeds and improved network coverage.

224.

The company has received numerous awards and recognition for its network reliability and customer service.

225.

Verizon has a strong presence in the sports industry, sponsoring major sporting events and partnering with professional sports teams.

226.

The company has been a key supporter of the NFL, sponsoring the Verizon Wireless Halftime Report and the NFL Mobile app.

227.

Verizon has invested in building smart city infrastructure, collaborating with municipalities to implement technologies that improve urban services and enhance connectivity.

228.

The company has made significant contributions to the advancement of telemedicine, enabling remote healthcare services and expanding access to medical professionals.

229.

Verizon's network played a critical role in enabling communication and providing support during natural disasters such as Hurricane Katrina and Superstorm Sandy.

230.

The company has a strong commitment to customer privacy and data security, implementing stringent measures to protect customer information.

231.

Verizon has been recognized as one of the top employers in the telecommunications industry, offering competitive benefits and opportunities for professional growth.

232.

The company has a history of supporting veterans and military personnel, providing job opportunities and resources through its military hiring initiatives.

233.

Verizon has been involved in various legal and regulatory battles throughout its history, including disputes over net neutrality and privacy regulations.

234.

In recent years, Verizon has expanded its focus beyond traditional telecommunications services, venturing into new areas such as digital media, advertising, and Internet of Things (IoT) solutions.

235.

The company has been actively involved in developing and promoting smart home technologies, offering services that allow customers to control and monitor their homes remotely.

236.

Verizon has partnered with academic institutions and research organizations to advance technological innovation and develop cutting-edge solutions.

237.

The company has supported educational initiatives, providing grants and resources to schools and universities to enhance STEM education.

238.

Verizon has been recognized for its commitment to sustainable business practices, receiving accolades for its environmental initiatives and transparency in reporting.

239.

The company has a strong commitment to accessibility, developing products and services that cater to the needs of individuals with disabilities.

240.

Verizon has made significant investments in fiber-optic networks, enabling faster and more reliable internet speeds for residential and business customers.

241.

The company has expanded its global presence through strategic partnerships and acquisitions, providing communication services to customers around the world.

242.

Verizon has been actively involved in promoting digital inclusion and bridging the digital divide by offering affordable internet access to underserved communities.

243.

The company has a strong focus on innovation and research, maintaining research and development facilities to drive technological advancements.

244.

Verizon has been a pioneer in the field of connected vehicles, partnering with automotive companies to develop and deploy technologies that enable safer and more efficient transportation.

245.

The company has been involved in the development of smart city initiatives, leveraging technology to improve urban infrastructure and enhance quality of life.

246.

Verizon has supported entrepreneurship and small business growth through various initiatives, providing resources and mentoring to aspiring entrepreneurs.

247.

The company has been recognized for its efforts in reducing its environmental footprint, including initiatives to reduce energy consumption and promote recycling.

248.

Verizon has been a leader in promoting digital safety and cybersecurity awareness, offering resources and educational materials to help customers protect their personal information.

249.

The company has a history of supporting cultural and artistic endeavors, sponsoring events and initiatives in the fields of music, theater, and visual arts.

250.

Verizon continues to evolve and adapt to the changing landscape of the telecommunications industry, striving to meet the evolving needs of its customers and provide innovative solutions for the future.

251.

PayPal was founded in December 1998 as Confinity by Max Levchin, Peter Thiel, and Luke Nosek.

252.

Originally, Confinity developed security software for handheld devices before shifting its focus to digital payments.

253.

In March 2000, Confinity merged with X.com, an online banking company founded by Elon Musk, who became the CEO of the merged entity.

254.

The merged company was renamed PayPal, reflecting its primary focus on online payment services.

255.

PayPal initially provided a payment platform for eBay, allowing users to securely buy and sell goods on the popular online auction site.

256.

PayPal's rapid growth in the early 2000s led to its initial public offering (IPO) in February 2002, making it a publicly traded company.

257.

eBay acquired PayPal in July 2002 for $1.5 billion, recognizing its potential to enhance the e-commerce experience on its platform.

258.

PayPal expanded beyond its initial partnership with eBay, allowing users to make online payments on various websites and in physical stores.

259.

PayPal became the leading online payment service, processing millions of transactions and facilitating international payments.

260.

In 2004, PayPal introduced its mobile payment solution, enabling users to send and receive money using their mobile devices.

261.

The success of PayPal attracted the attention of major financial institutions, and in 2005, PayPal was acquired by eBay's primary competitor, online marketplace operator, and payment processor, Braintree.

262.

PayPal continued to expand its services, offering additional features such as recurring payments, peer-to-peer payments, and the ability to link bank accounts and credit cards.

263.

In 2007, PayPal introduced the PayPal Here card reader, enabling small businesses to accept credit card payments using a mobile device.

264.

The company launched its "One Touch" feature in 2014, allowing users to make purchases with a single touch, eliminating the need for repetitive logins and password entries.

265.

PayPal expanded its global presence, entering new markets and supporting transactions in multiple currencies.

266.

In 2015, eBay spun off PayPal into a separate publicly traded company, recognizing the increasing importance of digital payments in the rapidly evolving e-commerce landscape.

267.

Following the spinoff, PayPal continued to innovate, introducing features such as PayPal Credit, which allows users to finance purchases.

268.

PayPal made strategic acquisitions to enhance its capabilities and expand its reach. Notable acquisitions include Braintree, Venmo, and Xoom Corporation.

269.

Venmo, acquired by PayPal in 2013, became popular among younger users for its social payment platform, enabling users to easily split bills and pay friends.

270.

PayPal's acquisition of Xoom Corporation in 2015 provided international money transfer capabilities, allowing users to send money to friends and family globally.

271.

The company made significant investments in security measures to protect users' financial information and prevent fraudulent activities.

272.

In 2018, PayPal introduced the ability to buy, hold, and sell cryptocurrencies, adding support for Bitcoin, Ethereum, Litecoin, and Bitcoin Cash.

273.

PayPal has been at the forefront of promoting financial inclusion, providing services to individuals and businesses who may not have access to traditional banking services.

274.

The company has been involved in various philanthropic initiatives, supporting organizations and projects that promote financial literacy and empowerment.

275.

PayPal's user base continued to expand, reaching hundreds of millions of active users worldwide.

276.

In 2020, PayPal announced its entry into the cryptocurrency market, allowing users to buy, sell, and hold cryptocurrencies directly within their PayPal accounts.

277.

The COVID-19 pandemic led to an increased reliance on digital payments, accelerating the adoption of PayPal's services.

278.

PayPal launched its "Pay in 4" feature in 2020,providing users with the option to split their purchases into four interest-free payments, making it easier for consumers to manage their budgets.

279.

The company has been a leader in advocating for digital wallets and contactless payments, supporting the shift towards a cashless society.

280.

PayPal has expanded its services to include support for online fundraising, allowing individuals and organizations to raise funds for charitable causes.

281.

The company has been involved in partnerships with major retailers and platforms, offering seamless payment experiences and exclusive discounts to PayPal users.

282.

PayPal has faced regulatory challenges and scrutiny over issues such as security, fraud prevention, and compliance with financial regulations.

283.

The company has implemented advanced fraud detection and prevention measures to protect its users and maintain the integrity of its platform.

284.

PayPal has been recognized for its commitment to environmental sustainability, implementing initiatives to reduce its carbon footprint and support renewable energy sources.

285.

The company has been an advocate for small businesses, providing tools and resources to help them thrive in the digital economy.

286.

PayPal has been involved in supporting entrepreneurs and startups through initiatives such as PayPal Start Tank, providing mentorship and financial support to promising ventures.

287.

The company has invested in technology and innovation, exploring emerging technologies such as blockchain and artificial intelligence to enhance its services.

288.

PayPal has played a significant role in enabling cross-border transactions, facilitating global commerce and empowering businesses to expand internationally.

289.

The company has been at the forefront of promoting digital financial services and financial inclusion in developing economies, providing opportunities for economic growth and empowerment.

290.

PayPal's brand recognition and reputation for security and reliability have made it a trusted and preferred payment method for consumers and businesses alike.

291.

The company has been recognized with numerous awards and accolades for its innovation, customer service, and corporate responsibility.

292.

PayPal has actively supported LGBTQ+ rights and equality, advocating for inclusive policies and promoting diversity and inclusion within the company.

293.

The company has a strong commitment to privacy and data protection, implementing robust security measures to safeguard user information.

294.

PayPal has been involved in partnerships and collaborations with government agencies and organizations to combat money laundering and financial crime.

295.

The company has actively supported disaster relief efforts, facilitating donations and financial assistance during times of crisis.

296.

PayPal's services have extended beyond online transactions, with partnerships in the offline retail sector, enabling users to make payments at physical stores using their PayPal accounts.

297.

The company has embraced the rise of digital wallets and payment platforms, participating in the open banking movement and fostering interoperability with other financial services providers.

298.

PayPal's innovative approach and continuous evolution have positioned it as a leader in the fintech industry, influencing the transformation of the payments landscape.

299.

The company has demonstrated resilience and adaptability in the face of changing market dynamics, evolving customer preferences, and emerging technologies.

300.

PayPal's history is marked by its commitment to simplifying and democratizing financial transactions, empowering individuals and businesses to participate in the digital economy with ease and security.

301.

Tao House, also known as the Eugene O'Neill National Historic Site, is located in Danville, California, USA.

302.

The house was the former residence of renowned playwright Eugene O'Neill and his wife, Carlotta Monterey.

303.

O'Neill lived at Tao House from 1937 to 1944, during which time he wrote some of his most celebrated plays, including "Long Day's Journey Into Night" and "The Iceman Cometh."

304.

Tao House is named after the Tao House Association, a nonprofit organization that played a crucial role in preserving and restoring the property.

305.

The house is situated on a secluded hillside, offering panoramic views of the surrounding landscape.

306.

Tao House was designated a National Historic Site in 1976, recognizing its significance in American literary and cultural history.

307.

The property consists of a main house, a cottage, and a garage, which have been restored to reflect their appearance during O'Neill's time.

308.

Visitors to Tao House can take guided tours to explore the interiors and learn about O'Neill's life and work.

309.

The rooms in the main house contain original furnishings, artwork, and personal belongings that belonged to O'Neill and Monterey.

310.

The study in the main house, where O'Neill wrote his plays, is one of the most significant and preserved spaces in the property.

311.

Tao House features a peaceful and serene garden, reflecting the playwright's affinity for nature and solitude.

312.

O'Neill chose to live at Tao House to escape distractions and focus on his writing in a quiet and secluded environment.

313.

The location of Tao House in the East Bay hills provided O'Neill with a tranquil setting and inspiration for his introspective and dramatic works.

314.

O'Neill and Monterey referred to Tao House as their "final harbor," where they sought refuge from the outside world.

315.

O'Neill's experiences and observations at Tao House greatly influenced the themes and characters in his plays.

316.

Tao House has been recognized as a gathering place for leading literary figures of the time, who visited O'Neill to discuss art, politics, and life.

317.

The property at Tao House includes a barn, which O'Neill converted into a rehearsal space for actors to perform his plays.

318.

The barn hosted intimate readings and rehearsals of O'Neill's works, allowing him to refine his plays before their public debut.

319.

The completion of several of O'Neill's major works, including "Long Day's Journey Into Night," occurred while he resided at Tao House.

320.

O'Neill's play "The Iceman Cometh" had its world premiere on Broadway in 1946, two years after his departure from Tao House.

321.

Tao House offers programs and events that celebrate O'Neill's legacy, including theatrical performances, lectures, and educational workshops.

322.

The property has an extensive archive of O'Neill's manuscripts, letters, and personal documents, which are preserved and accessible for research purposes.

323.

The Eugene O'Neill Foundation, in partnership with the National Park Service, manages and oversees the operations and programming at Tao House.

324.

Tao House welcomes visitors from around the world, attracting theater enthusiasts, scholars, and fans of Eugene O'Neill's works.

325.

The house and its surroundings offer a serene and reflective atmosphere, allowing visitors to connect with O'Neill's creative spirit and artistic journey.

326.

Tao House has been an inspiration for artists, writers, and playwrights, who draw upon O'Neill's life and the surrounding landscape for their own creative endeavors.

327.

The Eugene O'Neill Foundation conducts artist-in-residence programs at Tao House, providing an opportunity for emerging writers and artists to work in a setting that influenced O'Neill's artistic process.

328.

Tao House's architecture embodies a blend of Spanish Colonial Revivaland Mediterranean styles, characterized by stucco walls, red-tiled roofs, and arched doorways.

329.

The O'Neill family's decision to donate Tao House to the National Park Service was motivated by their desire to preserve O'Neill's legacy and make his works accessible to future generations.

330.

The Tao House Association played a vital role in raising funds and generating public support for the preservation and restoration of the property.

331.

Tao House provides a glimpse into O'Neill's personal life and the dynamics of his relationship with Carlotta Monterey, who played a significant role in his creative process and the management of his career.

332.

Eugene O'Neill's tenure at Tao House marked a period of introspection and self-discovery, during which he confronted personal demons and explored themes of family, love, and human suffering in his plays.

333.

Tao House's location in the Bay Area of California allowed O'Neill to stay connected to the vibrant cultural scene of San Francisco and its artistic community.

334.

The surrounding landscape of Tao House, with its rolling hills and oak trees, served as a source of solace and inspiration for O'Neill, influencing the naturalistic settings often found in his works.

335.

Eugene O'Neill's association with Tao House contributed to his recognition as one of America's greatest playwrights, earning him numerous accolades, including four Pulitzer Prizes for Drama.

336.

Tao House provides a glimpse into the daily routines and rituals of O'Neill and Monterey, giving visitors a sense of the creative atmosphere that permeated their lives.

337.

The preservation of Tao House allows visitors to witness the physical and emotional environment that shaped O'Neill's artistic vision and the development of his iconic plays.

338.

Tao House offers a retreat-like experience, inviting visitors to step back in time and immerse themselves in the world of Eugene O'Neill.

339.

The National Park Service provides interpretive tours at Tao House, where park rangers share insights into O'Neill's life, his works, and the significance of the property.

340.

Tao House serves as a reminder of the transformative power of creativity, showcasing the profound impact that a physical space can have on an artist's imagination and artistic output.

341.

The establishment of Tao House as a National Historic Site has fostered a greater understanding and appreciation of Eugene O'Neill's contributions to American theater and literature.

342.

The grounds surrounding Tao House are home to various native California plant species, offering a glimpse of the region's natural biodiversity.

343.

Tao House stands as a testament to the endurance and longevity of O'Neill's plays, which continue to be performed and studied worldwide.

344.

The Eugene O'Neill Foundation hosts an annual Eugene O'Neill Festival, featuring theatrical productions, lectures, and events that celebrate O'Neill's life and works.

345.

Tao House provides a serene environment for reflection and contemplation, inviting visitors to connect with O'Neill's profound exploration of the human condition.

346.

The legacy of Tao House extends beyond Eugene O'Neill's individual works, inspiring subsequent generations of playwrights and artists to push the boundaries of theatrical expression.

347.

The site offers a unique opportunity to explore the interplay between creativity and environment, shedding light on the profound influence of physical spaces on artistic endeavors.

348.

Tao House serves as a reminder of the importance of preserving cultural landmarks and historical sites that hold significance in the development of arts and culture.

349.

The impact of Tao House extends beyond its physical boundaries, with its influence felt in the theaters, classrooms, and artistic communities that continue to engage with O'Neill's plays.

350.

Tao House stands as a testament to the enduring legacy of Eugene O'Neill, a testament to the power of artistic expression, and an invitation for visitors to engage with the transformative power of theater and the written word.

351.

The Forty Acres was a historic film studio located in Culver City, California.

352.

It was originally built in 1926 by silent film producer Thomas Ince and named "Inceville."

353.

In 1928, Inceville was sold to Cecil B. DeMille, who renamed it "DeMille Studios."

354.

The studio covered 40 acres of land, hence its popular name, "The Forty Acres."

355.

The Forty Acres became one of the largest and most iconic film studios of the Golden Age of Hollywood.

356.

The studio was known for its versatile sets and backlots, which could be transformed to replicate various locations around the world.

357.

Many classic films and TV shows were filmed at The Forty Acres, including "Gone with the Wind," "The Wizard of Oz," and "The Andy Griffith Show."

358.

The famous "Hollywoodland" sign, originally erected to advertise a real estate development, was located on the hillside behind The Forty Acres.

359.

The studio boasted numerous sound stages, outdoor sets, and backlot streets, allowing for the creation of elaborate and realistic productions.

360.

The "New York Street" backlot set at The Forty Acres was one of the most frequently used sets, representing the bustling streets of New York City in many films and TV shows.

361.

The Forty Acres was known for its attention to detail and high production values, creating a realistic and immersive experience for audiences.

362.

In addition to film production, The Forty Acres also housed post-production facilities, including editing rooms and sound recording studios.

363.

The studio employed a large number of talented craftsmen, including set designers, carpenters, painters, and prop makers, who meticulously created and maintained the sets.

364.

The Forty Acres was home to the Desilu Productions company, founded by Lucille Ball and Desi Arnaz. They produced the popular TV series "I Love Lucy" and many other successful shows.

365.

The studio played a significant role in the development of the television industry, producing groundbreaking shows that defined the medium's early years.

366.

The Forty Acres had a reputation for being a creative and collaborative environment, attracting talented actors, directors, and writers.

367.

The studio lot often had multiple productions taking place simultaneously, with different crews working on various sets.

368.

The Forty Acres provided employment opportunities for thousands of people in the film and television industry, supporting the local economy.

369.

Many iconic film scenes were shot at The Forty Acres, including the "I'm melting!" scene from "The Wizard of Oz."

370.

The studio's outdoor sets and backlots were meticulously designed to create realistic and immersive environments, often fooling audiences into thinking they were filmed on location.

371.

The versatility of The Forty Acres allowed it to serve as the backdrop for a wide range of genres, from westerns to musicals to romantic comedies.

372.

The studio's success and reputation attracted international filmmakers, who chose to shoot their productions at The Forty Acres.

373.

The popularity of The Forty Acres made it a tourist attraction, with visitors coming to see the sets and possibly catch a glimpse of their favorite actors.

374.

The studio's backlot streets were meticulously maintained, with working lampposts, street signs, and storefronts, contributing to the realism of the productions.

375.

The Forty Acres often had specialized sets for specific genres, such as a western town, a city street, or a rural farm, allowing for efficient and seamless production.

376.

The studio had dedicated sound stages for interior scenes, equipped with state-of-the-art lighting and sound equipment.

377.

The Forty Acres was a hub of creativity and collaboration, with filmmakers and artists exchanging ideas and pushing the boundaries of storytelling.

378.

The studio was known for its commitment to innovation, embracing new technologies and techniques to enhance the filmmaking process.

379.

The Forty Acres had its own costume and wardrobe departments, responsible for creating and maintaining the elaborate costumes worn by actors in the productions.

380.

The studio's backlots were meticulously landscaped, with carefully chosen plants, trees, and flowers to create realistic and visually appealing environments.

381.

The scenic design team at The Forty Acres was renowned for their attention to detail, ensuring that every set piece and prop was historically accurate and visually stunning.

382.

The studio had its own film laboratories, where developed film negatives were processed and edited, ensuring the highest quality for the final productions.

383.

The Forty Acres attracted some of the biggest names in the entertainment industry, both in front of and behind the camera.

384.

The studio's reputation for excellence led to collaborations with renowned directors and producers, who sought to bring their creative visions to life at The Forty Acres.

385.

The studio was a hotbed of creativity, with writers, directors, and actors collaborating on scripts and performances to create memorable and impactful productions.

386.

The diverse range of sets and backlots at The Forty Acres allowed filmmakers to create fictional worlds and transport audiences to different eras and locations.

387.

The success of The Forty Acres contributed to the growth and popularity of the American film industry, shaping the cultural landscape of the 20th century.

388.

The decline of The Forty Acres can be attributed to the changing dynamics of the film industry, with studios shifting towards location shooting and smaller, independent productions.

389.

The rise of television and the advent of home video also had an impact on the studio's fortunes, as audiences had more entertainment options beyond traditional film releases.

390.

In 1976, The Forty Acres was sold to a real estate developer and subsequently demolished to make way for a residential and commercial development called "Raintree Plaza."

391.

The demolition of The Forty Acres marked the end of an era in Hollywood, with the loss of a significant piece of film history.

392.

Despite its physical disappearance, the legacy of The Forty Acres lives on in the countless films and television shows that were created within its walls.

393.

The iconic sets and backlots of The Forty Acres continue to influence filmmakers today, inspiring them to recreate the magic and authenticity that was once synonymous with the studio.

394.

The preservation and restoration of the history and memory of The Forty Acres is an ongoing endeavor, with efforts made to document its significance and educate future generations about its impact on the film industry.

395.

The story of The Forty Acres serves as a reminder of the ever-changing nature of the entertainment industry and the importance of preserving the heritage of film and television.

396.

The studio's legacy lives on in the memories of those who worked there and the films and TV shows that continue to entertain and captivate audiences.

397.

The creative spirit and collaborative energy that thrived at The Forty Acres continue to inspire filmmakers and artists, reminding them of the magic that can be created within the confines of a studio.

398.

The importance of The Forty Acres in the history of Hollywood is evident in its inclusion in discussions of the Golden Age of Hollywood and the development of the studio system.

399.

The architectural design and layout of The Forty Acres were carefully planned to maximize efficiency and accommodate the diverse needs of film production.

400.

The demise of The Forty Acres serves as a poignant reminder of the impermanence of physical structures and the fleeting nature of the entertainment industry, underscoring the need to document and preserve its history for future generations.

401.

The Galapagos lava heron (Butorides sundevalli) is a species of heron found exclusively in the Galapagos Islands.

402.

It is also known as the Galapagos striated heron or Galapagos green heron.

403.

The lava heron is relatively small, measuring around 45 centimeters in length.

404.

It has a distinct coloration with a dark bluish-gray back and wings, a lighter gray chest and belly, and a black cap on its head.

405.

The lava heron has long legs and a long, pointed beak, which it uses to catch small fish and crustaceans.

406.

It is primarily a solitary bird and is often seen perched on lava rocks along the shoreline, patiently waiting for prey to pass by.

407.

The lava heron is highly adapted to its volcanic habitat, where it blends in perfectly with the dark lava rocks.

408.

This species has a relatively limited distribution and is found on specific islands within the Galapagos archipelago, including Fernandina, Isabela, Santiago, and Santa Cruz.

409.

The lava heron is known for its agility and quick movements, allowing it to catch fast-moving prey in shallow water.

410.

It feeds on a variety of small aquatic creatures, including fish, crabs, shrimp, and insects.

411.

During the breeding season, which occurs between December and May, the male lava heron establishes a territory and performs elaborate courtship displays to attract a mate.

412.

The lava heron constructs its nest on the ground or in low vegetation, using twigs and other plant materials.

413.

The female lays a clutch of two to three eggs, which both parents take turns incubating for about 22 to 25 days.

414.

The chicks hatch covered in down feathers and are cared for by both parents until they fledge at around 30 to 35 days old.

415.

The lava heron faces few natural predators in its island habitat, although it may occasionally fall prey to large predatory birds such as hawks or owls.

416.

The species is considered to be of least concern in terms of conservation status, as it has a relatively stable population and a limited range.

417.

The lava heron plays an important ecological role in the Galapagos Islands by helping to control the populations of small fish and invertebrates.

418.

Its distribution across various islands within the archipelago indicates the bird's ability to adapt to different habitats and environmental conditions.

419.

The lava heron is well-adapted to foraging in rocky intertidal zones, where it can search for food among the crevices and pools of water.

420.

It is often observed using its sharp beak to spear prey and then quickly swallowing it whole.

421.

The lava heron has excellent eyesight, which aids in detecting and capturing small prey items.

422.

It is known to exhibit territorial behavior, defending its hunting grounds from other herons and birds.

423.

The lava heron's diet can vary depending on the availability of food sources, with crustaceans being a staple but also including small fish and insects.

424.

The bird's feeding strategy involves patience and stealth, remaining motionless for extended periods before striking at unsuspecting prey.

425.

The species has the ability to adapt its feeding behavior to different environments, displaying flexibility in its hunting techniques.

426.

The lava heron has been observed using tools, such as sticks or twigs, to lure prey out of crevices in rocks or to create a platform for easier access to food.

427.

This heron has a distinct vocalization, emitting a series of low, guttural croaks or a harsh squawk when disturbed or alarmed.

428.

The species is well-camouflaged among the volcanic rocks, providing it with protection from potential predators and allowing it to blend seamlessly into its surroundings.

429.

The lava heron has a relatively long lifespan, with individuals living up to 10 years or more in the wild.

430.

It is often associated with mangrove habitats, where it can find an abundant food supply and suitable nesting sites.

431.

The lava heron is a resilient species, adapted to the harsh and unpredictable environmental conditions of the Galapagos Islands, including volcanic activity and limited freshwater resources.

432.

It is a relatively sedentary species, with individuals typically staying within their established territories throughout the year.

433.

The lava heron's conservation status is influenced by various factors, including habitat destruction, disturbance by human activities, and potential introduction of invasive species to its island habitats.

434.

Efforts to protect and conserve the Galapagos Islands, including their unique ecosystems and wildlife, indirectly benefit the lava heron and other endemic species.

435.

The Galapagos lava heron's population size and distribution are closely monitored to ensure the species' long-term survival.

436.

The bird's adaptability and resilience have allowed it to thrive in a relatively limited range, showcasing its ability to adapt to the challenging conditions of the Galapagos Islands.

437.

The lava heron's distinct coloration and behavior make it a sought-after subject for wildlife photographers and birdwatchers visiting the Galapagos Islands.

438.

The species' presence serves as a reminder of the unique biodiversity found in the Galapagos archipelago and the importance of protecting these fragile ecosystems.

439.

The lava heron's role as a top predator in its habitat contributes to the ecological balance of the Galapagos Islands' coastal and marine ecosystems.

440.

This heron's ability to coexist with other bird species, such as the Galapagos mockingbird and lava gull, demonstrates the interconnectedness of species within the archipelago.

441.

The lava heron's small size allows it to navigate the rocky terrain and tight spaces of its habitat with agility and ease.

442.

The species has developed specific adaptations to withstand the extreme temperature fluctuations on the Galapagos Islands, including the ability to tolerate high heat and intense sunlight.

443.

The Galapagos lava heron is not migratory and has a relatively limited range, which adds to its vulnerability to changes in its habitat or threats to its local population.

444.

Climate change and sea-level rise pose potential risks to the lava heron's coastal habitats, as increased erosion and habitat loss could affect the availability of suitable foraging areas and nesting sites.

445.

The lava heron's presence in the Galapagos Islands serves as a living testament to the unique evolutionary processes that have shaped the archipelago's fauna and flora.

446.

The bird's adaptability and resilience reflect the incredible capacity of species to thrive in seemingly inhospitable environments.

447.

The lava heron's natural history and behavioral patterns continue to be studied by scientists and researchers to gain a better understanding of its ecological role and conservation needs.

448.

The species' specialized foraging techniques and ability to exploit different food sources demonstrate its ecological niche in the Galapagos Islands' complex food web.

449.

The conservation of the Galapagos lava heron is interconnected with broader conservation efforts focused on the protection and preservation of the archipelago's unique biodiversity.

450.

The lava heron's presence in the Galapagos Islands serves as a reminder of the ongoing importance of conservation measures to ensure the survival of this and other endemic species in this globally significant ecosystem.

451.

The Galapagos lava lizard (Microlophus spp.) is a group of endemic reptiles found exclusively in the Galapagos Islands.

452.

There are several species of lava lizards in the Galapagos, including the Galapagos lava lizard (Microlophus albemarlensis), Santa Fe lava lizard (Microlophus barringtonensis), and others.

453.

Lava lizards are small reptiles, typically measuring around 15-20 centimeters in length, with males being slightly larger than females.

454.

They have a slender body and a long tail, which they use for balance and communication.

455.

Lava lizards are known for their vibrant coloration, which can vary depending on the species and the individual. They often display combinations of green, brown, black, and orange hues.

456.

The coloration of lava lizards helps them blend into their volcanic habitat, providing camouflage from predators and prey.

457.

Male lava lizards have a distinctive, brightly colored throat patch known as a "dewlap." They use this dewlap during territorial displays and courtship rituals.

458.

The dewlap of male lava lizards can change color, becoming more vibrant during displays of aggression or courtship.

459.

Lava lizards are diurnal, meaning they are active during the day and rest at night.

460.

They are primarily insectivorous, feeding on a variety of small insects such as beetles, ants, and spiders.

461.

Lava lizards are agile climbers and can often be seen perched on rocks, trees, or cacti, scanning their surroundings for prey.

462.

The reproductive behavior of lava lizards is complex. Males establish territories and engage in elaborate displays to attract females.

463.

The male lava lizards perform push-up displays, head-bobbing, and vigorous tail movements to impress potential mates.

464.

Females lay their eggs in shallow nests dug into the sandy or volcanic soil.

465.

Lava lizard eggs are typically buried to protect them from predators and temperature fluctuations.

466.

After an incubation period of several weeks, the eggs hatch, and the young lizards emerge.

467.

Lava lizards exhibit sexual dimorphism, with males being larger and more brightly colored than females.

468.

The size and coloration of male lava lizards are important indicators of their social status and reproductive success.

469.

Lava lizards have adapted to the challenging volcanic environment of the Galapagos Islands. They can tolerate high temperatures and rocky terrain.

470.

They are excellent climbers and are capable of scaling steep volcanic slopes with ease.

471.

Lava lizards play an important role in the ecosystem as both predators and prey. They control insect populations while serving as a food source for birds and other predators.

472.

The different species of lava lizards in the Galapagos Islands have specific adaptations to their respective habitats and diets.

473.

Lava lizards are highly territorial and defend their territories from intruding males. Territory size varies depending on factors such as resource availability and population density.

474.

The lava lizards' ability to regulate their body temperature allows them to thrive in the extreme heat of the Galapagos Islands.

475.

Lava lizards are known for their swift movements and agility, which help them evade predators and capture prey.

476.

They have excellent eyesight and rely on visual cues to detect predators and locate potential mates.

477.

The social hierarchy among male lava lizards is established through aggressive displays and territorial behavior.

478.

Lava lizards are capable of regenerating their tails if they are injured or severed.

479.

The regeneration process of a lizard's tail involves the growth of new tissue and the development of cartilage and scales.

480.

Lava lizards have been studied extensively by scientists interested in the evolution and adaptation of species in isolated island ecosystems.

481.

The isolation of the Galapagos Islands has led to the formation of distinct species of lava lizards, each adapted to specific ecological niches.

482.

The genetic diversity of lava lizards in the Galapagos Islands provides valuable insights into the processes of speciation and evolution.

483.

Lava lizards have been found on various islands in the Galapagos archipelago, including Fernandina, Isabela, Santa Cruz, and others.

484.

Lava lizards are relatively common in the Galapagos Islands and are frequently encountered by visitors exploring the unique habitats of the archipelago.

485.

The presence of lava lizards in certain habitats can indicate the health and stability of the ecosystem, as they are sensitive to environmental changes.

486.

The conservation status of lava lizards varies depending on the specific species and their respective island distributions.

487.

Some species of lava lizards are considered vulnerable or endangered due to habitat destruction, introduced predators, and competition with invasive species.

488.

The Galapagos National Park and other conservation organizations work to protect the habitats of lava lizards and implement measures to minimize human impacts.

489.

Lava lizards are popular subjects for scientific research, as they provide valuable information about the processes of adaptation, evolution, and island biogeography.

490.

The presence of lava lizards in the Galapagos Islands serves as a reminder of the unique and fragile ecosystems that exist within the archipelago.

491.

Their adaptability and resilience highlight the incredible capacity of species to thrive in isolated and challenging environments.

492.

The study of lava lizards contributes to our understanding of the ecological dynamics and evolutionary processes occurring in the Galapagos Islands.

493.

Lava lizards are an integral part of the Galapagos Islands' biodiversity, showcasing the complex interactions between species and their environments.

494.

The conservation of lava lizards aligns with broader efforts to protect and preserve the unique flora and fauna of the Galapagos archipelago.

495.

The presence of lava lizards in the Galapagos Islands offers visitors the opportunity to observe and appreciate the diverse wildlife that has evolved in isolation over millions of years.

496.

The Galapagos Islands, with their lava lizards and other endemic species, serve as a living laboratory for the study of evolution and the interconnectedness of species.

497.

Lava lizards are an iconic symbol of the Galapagos Islands and are often featured in documentaries, photographs, and artwork depicting the unique wildlife of the archipelago.

498.

The study of lava lizards contributes to our understanding of the processes shaping biodiversity and provides insights into the effects of environmental changes on island ecosystems.

499.

The conservation of lava lizards involves addressing factors such as habitat degradation, invasive species control, and the promotion of sustainable tourism practices.

500.

The continued conservation of lava lizards in the Galapagos Islands ensures the preservation of their unique genetic heritage and contributes to the overall biodiversity and ecological health of the archipelago.

501.

Intel Corporation, commonly known as Intel, is an American multinational technology company and one of the world's largest semiconductor chip manufacturers.

502.

Intel was founded on July 18, 1968, by Robert Noyce and Gordon Moore. They were joined by Andrew Grove, who became a key figure in the company's history.

503.

The name "Intel" is derived from the words "integrated" and "electronics," reflecting the company's focus on integrated circuit technology.

504.

Intel's first product was the 3101 Schottky TTL bipolar memory chip, released in 1969. It was the world's first commercially available metal-oxide-semiconductor (MOS) chip.

505.

In 1971, Intel introduced the Intel 4004 microprocessor, which was the first commercially available microprocessor and revolutionized the computing industry.

506.

The Intel 4004 microprocessor paved the way for the development of personal computers, as it enabled the integration of multiple electronic components onto a single chip.

507.

Intel continued to innovate in the microprocessor market, introducing the 8008 and 8080 microprocessors, which further expanded the capabilities of early computer systems.

508.

The breakthrough moment for Intel came in 1978 with the introduction of the Intel 8086 microprocessor, which served as the foundation for the x86 architecture that still dominates the computer industry today.

509.

Intel's x86 architecture became the industry standard for microprocessors and was adopted by numerous computer manufacturers.

510.

In the 1980s, Intel faced fierce competition from other microprocessor manufacturers, such as Motorola and Zilog, but emerged as the market leader due to its superior technology and strategic partnerships.

511.

In 1983, Intel released the 80286 microprocessor, which offered significant performance improvements over its predecessors and further solidified the company's dominance in the PC market.

512.

The 1990s saw Intel's rise to prominence with the release of the Pentium series of microprocessors, which became synonymous with high-performance computing.

513.

The "Intel Inside" marketing campaign, launched in 1991, played a crucial role in promoting the Intel brand and creating consumer awareness about the importance of microprocessors in computers.

514.

Intel's focus expanded beyond microprocessors, and the company began producing a wide range of semiconductor products, including memory chips, network processors, and graphics processing units (GPUs).

515.

In 1997, Intel formed a strategic alliance with Hewlett-Packard to develop the Itanium microprocessor architecture, targeting high-performance computing and enterprise markets.

516.

Intel faced significant competition in the early 2000s with the emergence of Advanced Micro Devices (AMD), which introduced competitive microprocessors.

517.

In response to this competition, Intel accelerated its pace of innovation and released a series of successful microprocessor families, including the Core series and the Xeon series for servers and workstations.

518.

In 2006, Intel made a significant shift in its microprocessor architecture by introducing the Intel Core microarchitecture, which offered improved performance and energy efficiency.

519.

Intel's manufacturing prowess and advanced semiconductor fabrication processes, such as the introduction of 22nm, 14nm, and 10nm process technologies, further solidified its technological leadership.

520.

The company's success extended beyond microprocessors, with Intel expanding into new areas such as wireless communication, artificial intelligence, autonomous driving, and cloud computing.

521.

In 2005, Intel joined forces with Apple to transition Mac computers from PowerPC processors to Intel processors, which marked a significant shift in the industry and boosted Intel's market presence.

522.

Intel faced numerous legal challenges over the years, including antitrust lawsuits and accusations of anti-competitive practices, particularly related to its dominance in the microprocessor market.

523.

Intel's involvement in research and development has been significant, with the company investing heavily in advancing semiconductor technology and driving innovation.

524.

Intel has a strong commitment to education and community development, supporting various initiatives and programs to promote STEM education and empower underprivileged communities.

525.

The company has been recognized for its environmental sustainability efforts, including reducing its carbon footprint, promoting energy efficiency, and responsible waste management.

526.

In recent years, Intel has faced increasing competition from rival semiconductor manufacturers, particularly in the mobile and tablet markets, where ARM-based processors dominate.

527.

The rise of mobile computing and the decline in PC sales have posed challenges for Intel, leading the company to diversify its product offerings and explore new markets.

528.

In 2011, Intel acquired McAfee, a leading cybersecurity company, to enhance its security offerings and protect against emerging threats.

529.

Intel has a long-standing partnership with the International Olympic Committee (IOC) and has been an official Olympic partner, providing technological support and innovations for the Olympic Games.

530.

In 2020, Intel announced its entry into the discrete graphics card market, with the launch of the Intel Xe architecture, aiming to compete with industry giants like NVIDIA and AMD.

531.

Intel has a strong presence worldwide, with offices and manufacturing facilities in numerous countries, including the United States, China, Israel, India, and Ireland.

532.

The company is known for its rigorous "tick-tock" development model, where it alternates between introducing a new microarchitecture ("tock") and refining the manufacturing process ("tick") every two years.

533.

Intel's annual revenue has consistently been in the tens of billions of dollars, making it one of the largest and most influential technology companies globally.

534.

The company's success has made it a significant contributor to the United States' economy and a symbol of American technological innovation.

535.

Over the years, Intel has actively acquired various technology companies to enhance its product portfolio and expand into new markets. Notable acquisitions include Altera, Mobileye, and Nervana Systems.

536.

Intel has a long history of collaborating with academic institutions, research organizations, and industry partners to drive advancements in technology and address complex technological challenges.

537.

The company has received numerous accolades and awards for its technological advancements, innovation, and corporate social responsibility initiatives.

538.

Intel has made significant contributions to the development of open-source software and actively supports the open-source community.

539.

Intel's commitment to diversity and inclusion is reflected in its efforts to create an inclusive work environment and promote diversity throughout its workforce and leadership positions.

540.

The company has a strong commitment to corporate social responsibility, investing in initiatives that promote sustainability, education, and community engagement.

541.

In 2019, Intel announced its ambitious goal to achieve "net positive" water use, meaning it aims to restore more water than it consumes in its operations by 2030.

542.

Intel has been at the forefront of technological advancements, playing a key role in driving the development of Moore's Law, which states that the number of transistors on a microchip doubles approximately every two years.

543.

The company has established multiple Intel Labs around the world, dedicated to conducting advanced research and development in areas such as artificial intelligence and machine learning, quantum computing, and advanced materials.

544.

Intel has actively contributed to the development of industry standards, collaborating with other technology companies to ensure compatibility and interoperability across different hardware and software platforms.

545.

The company's commitment to customer-centric innovation is reflected in its continuous efforts to improve performance, power efficiency, and security in its microprocessor designs.

546.

Intel has a strong commitment to ethical business practices and has implemented strict policies and guidelines to ensure compliance with legal and regulatory requirements.

547.

The company has weathered several economic downturns and market fluctuations over its history, demonstrating resilience and adaptability in the face of changing industry dynamics.

548.

Intel's corporate culture fosters a spirit of innovation and collaboration, encouraging employees to think creatively and push the boundaries of technology.

549.

The company's commitment to sustainability extends to its supply chain, where it works closely with suppliers to promote responsible sourcing and environmental stewardship.

550.

Intel's influence on the technology industry is undeniable, as its microprocessors power a significant portion of the world's computers, servers, and data centers, driving advancements in computing and shaping the digital landscape.

551.

Mattel, Inc. is an American multinational toy manufacturing company, known for its iconic brands such as Barbie, Hot Wheels, and Fisher-Price.

552.

Mattel was founded in 1945 by Harold "Matt" Matson and Elliot Handler in a garage workshop in Southern California.

553.

The name "Mattel" is a combination of the founders' names, Matson and Elliot.

554.

Initially, Mattel produced picture frames before transitioning to manufacturing dollhouse furniture.

555.

In 1955, Mattel introduced its first toy hit, the "Burp Gun," a cap gun that made a realistic burping sound.

556.

Mattel's breakthrough came in 1959 with the introduction of Barbie, created by Ruth Handler, Elliot Handler's wife. Barbie quickly became one of the most iconic and best-selling toys of all time.

557.

Barbie was named after the Handlers' daughter, Barbara. It was the first adult-bodied fashion doll aimed at girls, challenging the market dominated by baby dolls.

558.

In the 1960s, Mattel expanded its product line by acquiring other toy companies, including Chatty Cathy dolls and Matchbox cars.

559.

In 1968, Mattel launched Hot Wheels, a line of die-cast toy cars with innovative features like working suspension and super-fast wheels.

Hot Wheels became an instant success and a fierce competitor to Matchbox.

560.

Mattel's success continued in the 1970s with the introduction of more popular toy lines, such as the talking doll "Baby First Step" and the handheld electronic game "Football."

561.

The 1980s brought Mattel further success with the release of the Masters of the Universe toy line, which included action figures, playsets, and an accompanying animated TV series.

562.

In the 1990s, Mattel acquired The Learning Company, a leading educational software company, in an effort to expand into the interactive and digital entertainment market.

563.

In 1997, Mattel faced a significant setback when it introduced a talking Barbie that said phrases like "Math class is tough." The doll faced criticism for perpetuating negative stereotypes about girls and their abilities.

564.

Mattel weathered the controversy and continued to innovate with new products, such as the interactive virtual pet toy "Poo-Chi" and the digital camera for kids called "Kidizoom."

565.

Mattel acquired Fisher-Price, a well-known brand specializing in toys for infants and young children, in 1993. Fisher-Price became a subsidiary of Mattel.

566.

Mattel expanded its global presence by establishing manufacturing facilities and sales offices in various countries worldwide.

567.

The early 2000s brought new challenges to Mattel, as the company faced recalls of millions of toys due to safety concerns, particularly related to lead paint and small parts.

568.

Mattel took immediate action to improve safety standards and enhance product testing and monitoring procedures, working closely with regulatory agencies to address the issues.

569.

In 2009, Mattel celebrated Barbie's 50th anniversary with various events and collaborations, showcasing Barbie's enduring cultural influence and iconic status.

570.

Mattel continued to introduce new toy lines and expand its brand portfolio, acquiring popular franchises such as Thomas & Friends, American Girl, and the licensing rights for Disney Princess and Pixar characters.

571.

In recent years, Mattel has embraced technological advancements, incorporating interactive features into its toys, such as app connectivity and augmented reality experiences.

572.

Mattel has collaborated with other major brands and entertainment properties, including collaborations with DC Comics, WWE, and Jurassic World, to create licensed toys and merchandise.

573.

The company has prioritized sustainability and environmental responsibility, aiming to use 100% recycled, recyclable, or bio-based plastic materials in its products and packaging by 2030.

574.

Mattel has been recognized for its efforts in diversity and inclusion, launching a variety of Barbie dolls representing different ethnicities, body types, and professions to promote inclusivity and inspire children.

575.

Mattel's commitment to corporate social responsibility is evident through its philanthropic initiatives, including partnerships with organizations like the Special Olympics and Save the Children.

576.

Mattel has expanded its entertainment division, creating content based on its popular toy brands, including animated series, movies, and digital media.

577.

The company has embraced e-commerce and digital marketing, utilizing online platforms and social media to engage with consumers and promote its products.

578.

Mattel has faced challenges from changing consumer preferences, such as the shift towards digital entertainment and video games, which has impacted traditional toy sales.

579.

To adapt to changing market dynamics, Mattel has ventured into new avenues, such as creating content for streaming platforms and developing interactive gaming experiences.

580.

Mattel has collaborated with technology companies to incorporate emerging technologies like virtual reality and artificial intelligence into its products, offering interactive and immersive play experiences.

581.

Mattel has a strong presence in the global toy market, with distribution networks and retail partnerships spanning numerous countries.

582.

The company has been recognized for its toy design and innovation, receiving numerous awards and accolades, including the prestigious Toy of the Year awards.

583.

Mattel has faced competition from other major toy manufacturers, such as Hasbro and LEGO, in the fiercely competitive toy industry.

584.

The company has adapted to the changing retail landscape, expanding its online presence and partnering with e-commerce platforms to reach a broader customer base.

585.

Mattel's iconic brands have become cultural touchstones, inspiring generations of children and collectors around the world.

586.

The Barbie brand, in particular, has evolved to reflect changing societal norms and has been celebrated for promoting positive self-image and empowerment for girls.

587.

Mattel has a dedicated team of designers, engineers, and innovators who work tirelessly to create toys that engage and inspire children's imaginations.

588.

The company has established the Mattel Children's Foundation, which focuses on philanthropic efforts to support children's health, education, and well-being globally.

589.

Mattel has been recognized as one of the world's most ethical companies by the Ethisphere Institute, highlighting its commitment to ethical business practices and corporate governance.

590.

The Mattel PlayBack program, launched in 2020, allows consumers to send back their old Mattel toys for recycling, demonstrating the company's commitment to sustainability and reducing environmental impact.

591.

Mattel has collaborated with renowned designers and fashion brands to create limited-edition collectible dolls and designer collaborations, such as the Barbie x Christian Siriano collection.

592.

The company has a strong licensing program, partnering with popular franchises and brands to create toys and merchandise based on beloved characters and properties.

593.

Mattel has established partnerships with educational institutions and organizations to support research and development in the fields of child development and play.

594.

The company has a rich history of memorable advertising campaigns, including the iconic "Barbie Girl" song by Aqua, which became a global hit in the late 1990s.

595.

Mattel has embraced social and environmental responsibility by implementing sustainable sourcing practices and reducing its carbon footprint across its supply chain.

596.

The company has actively engaged in diversity and inclusion initiatives, both in its workforce and in the toys it creates, to ensure representation and inclusivity for all children.

597.

Mattel has a dedicated team of toy safety experts who work diligently to ensure that its products meet or exceed rigorous safety standards and regulations.

598.

The company has established the Mattel Children's Hospital UCLA, a leading pediatric facility that provides specialized healthcare services for children.

599.

Mattel's toys have become iconic cultural artifacts, with some vintage and rare toys becoming highly sought-after collectibles among enthusiasts and collectors.

600.

Throughout its history, Mattel has remained committed to its mission of creating innovative, engaging, and high-quality toys that bring joy and inspire imagination in children worldwide.

601.

The Tule Lake Segregation Center was a World War II-era internment camp located in Modoc County, California, United States.

602.

The camp was initially established as the Tule Lake War Relocation Center in 1942 to incarcerate Japanese Americans and Japanese immigrants considered a "potential threat" to national security.

603.

The Tule Lake Segregation Center was the largest and most controversial of the ten internment camps established by the U.S. government during the war.

604.

At its peak, the Tule Lake camp held over 18,000 Japanese Americans, making it one of the largest population centers in Northern California at the time.

605.

The camp was situated on the former Tule Lakebed, a dry lakebed located in a remote and desolate area of California's high desert.

606.

Tule Lake was initially intended to be a temporary relocation center, but it later became a segregation center due to the high number of dissidents and individuals deemed "disloyal" by the U.S. government.

607.

The designation as a segregation center meant that Tule Lake housed individuals who refused to swear loyalty to the United States or expressed dissent towards the government's actions.

608.

The internment of Japanese Americans at Tule Lake was a result of Executive Order 9066, signed by President Franklin D. Roosevelt, which authorized the forced relocation and internment of individuals of Japanese ancestry during World War II.

609.

Tule Lake became known for its high-security measures, including multiple barbed wire fences, guard towers, and military police patrols.

610.

The camp was surrounded by an additional eight-foot-tall barbed wire fence, creating a double perimeter security system.

611.

Tule Lake was also home to a stockade, where dissidents and those who resisted internment were held under military guard.

612.

In November 1943, the U.S. government established the Tule Lake Segregation Center as a separate entity from other internment camps due to its large population of "disloyal" individuals.

613.

Tule Lake became a center for protest and resistance against the internment and discriminatory policies, with many inmates demanding better treatment and civil rights.

614.

The camp was the site of several strikes and demonstrations, with inmates advocating for fair treatment, better living conditions, and the restoration of their constitutional rights.

615.

Tule Lake was also known for its vibrant cultural and intellectual life, with prisoners forming community organizations, creating art, and organizing educational programs within the camp.

616.

The Tule Lake camp had its own newspaper called the Tulean Dispatch, which provided information and news to the inmates and documented their experiences.

617.

The Tule Lake Segregation Center had a complex social and political structure, with various factions emerging based on different political beliefs and levels of allegiance to the U.S. government.

618.

The segregation of "disloyal" individuals at Tule Lake had profound impacts on families, with many being separated or divided based on their responses to loyalty questionnaires.

619.

The segregation center housed individuals from diverse backgrounds, including those born in the United States (Nisei) and those who were immigrants (Issei).

620.

In 1944, the War Department established the Tule Lake All-Citizen Civilian Service Corps, which allowed inmates to work outside the camp on public works projects, such as constructing irrigation canals and roads.

621.

Tule Lake was the only internment camp where the U.S. government built a maximum-security jail, known as the "Ironwood Jail," for holding inmates deemed particularly dangerous or disruptive.

622.

The incarceration of Japanese Americans at Tule Lake and other internment camps was widely criticized as a violation of civil liberties and constitutional rights.

623.

The Tule Lake Segregation Center was officially closed in March 1946, and the remaining inmates were released or transferred to other facilities.

624.

After the closure of the camp, the Tule Lake site was primarily used for agricultural purposes, with former camp buildings repurposed or demolished.

625.

In the 1970s, efforts began to recognize the historical significance of Tule Lake and preserve the site as a reminder of the injustice and trauma experienced by Japanese Americans during World War II.

626.

The Tule Lake Segregation Center is now recognized as a National Historic Landmark and is part of the Tule Lake Unit of the World War II Valor in the Pacific National Monument.

627.

The site includes various historical markers, interpretive panels, and remnants of camp structures, providing visitors with insights into the experiences of those interned at Tule Lake.

628.

The Tule Lake camp represents a painful chapter in American history and serves as a reminder of the consequences of wartime hysteria, racism, and the erosion of civil liberties.

629.

In 2008, the National Park Service conducted an extensive archaeological survey at the Tule Lake site, uncovering artifacts that shed light on daily life in the camp.

630.

Tule Lake has been the subject of artistic and literary works, including novels, memoirs, documentaries, and films, that aim to raise awareness about the internment experience.

631.

The Tule Lake Pilgrimage, an annual event organized by former incarcerees, their families, and supporters, takes place at the Tule Lake site to remember and reflect on the internment experience.

632.

In recent years, efforts have been made to preserve and restore the remaining buildings at Tule Lake to provide a more comprehensive historical understanding of the camp's layout and conditions.

633.

The Tule Lake Preservation Committee, formed by former incarcerees and their descendants, works to preserve the history and memory of Tule Lake and advocate for its recognition as a site of conscience.

634.

The Tule Lake National Monument Act was signed into law in December 2020, designating the Tule Lake site as a unit of the National Park System, ensuring its preservation and interpretation for future generations.

635.

The Tule Lake Segregation Center serves as a reminder of the resilience and strength of the Japanese American community, who persevered in the face of adversity and fought for justice and civil rights.

636.

The incarceration experience at Tule Lake and other internment camps prompted significant changes in U.S. policies and attitudes towards civil rights, leading to redress and reparations for Japanese Americans in the 1980s.

637.

Tule Lake has become a site of pilgrimage and remembrance, attracting visitors from around the world who seek to understand the history of Japanese American internment and learn from past injustices.

638.

The Tule Lake site provides opportunities for educational programs and research, promoting dialogue and understanding about the experiences of Japanese Americans during World War II.

639.

Efforts are underway to gather and preserve oral histories of former Tule Lake incarcerees, ensuring that their voices and stories are recorded for future generations.

640.

Tule Lake serves as a cautionary reminder of the importance of upholding civil liberties, protecting human rights, and combating prejudice and discrimination in times of national crisis.

641.

The history of Tule Lake has sparked discussions and debates about the balance between national security and individual rights, highlighting the importance of a vigilant and inclusive democracy.

642.

The legacy of Tule Lake continues to resonate, influencing contemporary discussions on social justice, immigrant rights, and the treatment of marginalized communities.

643.

The Tule Lake Segregation Center stands as a physical manifestation of the internment experience, fostering empathy and understanding for the injustices faced by Japanese Americans during World War II.

644.

The ongoing research and documentation of Tule Lake's history contribute to the broader understanding of the impacts of wartime internment on individuals, families, and communities.

645.

Tule Lake has been the subject of academic research and scholarship, shedding light on various aspects of the internment experience, including resistance, identity, and community dynamics.

646.

The Tule Lake site provides opportunities for visitors to engage in dialogue, reflection, and commemoration, fostering a commitment to human rights, social justice, and the prevention of similar injustices in the future.

647.

The story of Tule Lake extends beyond the confines of the camp, influencing broader narratives of immigration, exclusion, and the pursuit of justice in American history.

648.

Tule Lake serves as a symbol of resilience and the power of collective memory, reminding society of the importance of preserving historical sites and stories to ensure a more just and inclusive future.

649.

The experiences and lessons learned from Tule Lake have inspired activism and advocacy for civil rights, promoting a society that values diversity, inclusivity, and equal treatment for all.

650.

The ongoing recognition and commemoration of Tule Lake encourage continued dialogue and examination of the past, reinforcing the commitment to ensure that such injustices are not repeated in the future.

651.

The Twenty-Five-Foot Space Simulator (TFSS) is a large-scale testing facility located at NASA's Plum Brook Station in Ohio, United States.

652.

The TFSS is one of the largest vacuum chambers in the world, standing 25 feet (7.6 meters) tall and measuring 100 feet (30 meters) in diameter.

653.

The primary purpose of the TFSS is to simulate the space environment for testing spacecraft, satellites, and their components under conditions similar to those encountered in space.

654.

The simulator's vacuum chamber can be evacuated to extremely low pressure levels, reaching as low as 1×10^{-6} torr, which is equivalent to the near-vacuum conditions of outer space.

655.

The TFSS is capable of recreating extreme temperature variations, ranging from extremely cold temperatures as low as -250 degrees Fahrenheit (-157 degrees Celsius) to high temperatures approaching 200 degrees Fahrenheit (93 degrees Celsius).

656.

The simulator is equipped with powerful thermal shrouds and liquid nitrogen cooling systems to create the extreme temperature conditions necessary for testing.

657.

The TFSS can simulate the vacuum of space and the solar radiation encountered in orbit, allowing engineers to evaluate the performance and durability of spacecraft materials and systems.

658.

The simulator's large size accommodates the testing of full-scale spacecraft or spacecraft components, providing a realistic environment for evaluation.

659.

The TFSS is frequently used for testing spacecraft propulsion systems, such as rocket engines and thrusters, to ensure their performance and reliability in space.

660.

In addition to propulsion systems, the simulator is used to test various spacecraft subsystems, including solar panels, antennas, instruments, and structural components.

661.

The TFSS has been instrumental in testing and qualifying numerous NASA missions, including the Hubble Space Telescope, the Mars rovers, the Lunar Module, and the International Space Station (ISS).

662.

The simulator is capable of simulating the conditions encountered during launch, as it can subject spacecraft to high levels of vibration and acoustic stress to evaluate their structural integrity.

663.

The TFSS's unique capabilities allow engineers to simulate the harsh conditions of space and conduct thorough testing on spacecraft before they are launched, reducing the risk of failure during missions.

664.

The facility is equipped with a sophisticated data acquisition system that records and analyzes various parameters, such as temperature, pressure, vibration, and electromagnetic compatibility, during testing.

665.

The TFSS provides engineers with valuable data on the behavior of spacecraft materials and systems under simulated space conditions, aiding in the design and improvement of future missions.

666.

The simulator's testing capabilities extend beyond spacecraft components to include experiments and research in fields such as astrophysics, materials science, and life sciences.

667.

The TFSS can be configured to simulate different orbital environments, including low Earth orbit, geostationary orbit, and interplanetary space, enabling a wide range of testing scenarios.

668.

The facility features a sophisticated control room where engineers and technicians monitor and control the testing process, adjusting parameters and ensuring the safety of the equipment and personnel.

669.

The TFSS is part of NASA's Glenn Research Center, which focuses on advanced technology development and testing for space exploration and aeronautics.

670.

Construction of the TFSS began in the 1960s, and the facility became operational in 1969. It has since undergone several upgrades and improvements to enhance its testing capabilities.

671.

The TFSS is often used in conjunction with other testing facilities at Plum Brook Station, such as the Space Power Facility, to provide comprehensive testing capabilities for large spacecraft and systems.

672.

The simulator's location at Plum Brook Station offers a secluded and controlled environment, minimizing external disturbances and ensuring the accuracy of test results.

673.

The TFSS's testing capabilities have attracted international collaborations, with space agencies and industry partners from around the world utilizing the facility for their testing needs.

674.

In addition to NASA missions, the TFSS has supported testing for commercial space companies, including SpaceX, Blue Origin, and Boeing, as they develop and qualify their spacecraft and launch systems.

675.

The TFSS has played a crucial role in advancing space exploration and technology development by enabling rigorous testing and validation of spacecraft systems and components.

676.

The simulator's unique capabilities have contributed to the success of numerous space missions, enabling spacecraft to withstand the demanding conditions of space and fulfill their scientific and exploration objectives.

677.

The TFSS has a highly skilled workforce, including engineers, technicians, and scientists, who specialize in designing and conducting tests to meet the specific needs of each mission.

678.

The facility's testing protocols and procedures undergo stringent quality control measures to ensure the accuracy and reliability of test data.

679.

The TFSS has been used to study the effects of space radiation on materials, electronics, and biological samples, aiding in the development of radiation shielding and protection for future space missions.

680.

The simulator's capabilities allow for long-duration testing, simulating the extended exposure to the space environment that spacecraft experience during their operational lifetimes.

681.

The TFSS is equipped with specialized lighting systems to replicate the solar spectrum and simulate the illumination conditions encountered in space.

682.

The facility's versatile design allows for quick reconfiguration and adaptation to accommodate various testing requirements, optimizing efficiency and enabling a wide range of experiments.

683.

The TFSS provides a controlled environment for testing satellite communications systems, evaluating signal propagation, interference, and performance under simulated space conditions.

684.

The simulator has been used to validate and optimize the performance of advanced space telescopes, such as the James Webb Space Telescope, ensuring their precision and accuracy for astronomical observations.

685.

The TFSS has supported research on the effects of microgravity on plant growth and development, contributing to advancements in space agriculture and future long-duration space missions.

686.

The simulator's vacuum chamber is made of durable materials, such as stainless steel, to withstand the extreme conditions and maintain a high level of vacuum integrity.

687.

The TFSS's testing capabilities have expanded to include CubeSats and small satellite systems, enabling the evaluation of these compact and innovative spacecraft designs.

688.

The facility has state-of-the-art safety systems and protocols in place to protect personnel and equipment during testing, ensuring a safe working environment.

689.

The TFSS has played a critical role in the advancement of space technology and the development of new materials and manufacturing processes for use in space exploration.

690.

The simulator's capabilities support research on the effects of long-duration space missions on human health and well-being, aiding in the development of countermeasures and mitigations for future crewed missions.

691.

The TFSS has a legacy of supporting critical testing needs for NASA's human spaceflight programs, ensuring the safety and reliability of crewed spacecraft like the Space Shuttle and the upcoming Artemis missions to the Moon.

692.

The facility's location within the Plum Brook Station complex provides access to other specialized testing facilities, expertise, and resources, fostering a collaborative environment for space exploration research and development.

693.

The TFSS has contributed to the advancement of materials science by facilitating experiments on the behavior of different materials under extreme temperature, vacuum, and radiation conditions.

694.

The simulator's testing capabilities are not limited to spacecraft systems but also extend to scientific instruments, payloads, and experiments destined for space missions.

695.

The TFSS has been instrumental in advancing the understanding of spacecraft contamination and outgassing, helping to ensure the cleanliness and integrity of sensitive instruments and optics in space.

696.

The facility has supported testing for Mars exploration missions, including the Viking landers, Mars rovers, and the upcoming Mars Sample Return mission, enabling scientists and engineers to study the behavior of spacecraft and instruments in simulated Martian environments.

697.

The TFSS has been used to test and validate the performance of propulsion systems for deep space missions, such as the Voyager spacecraft, which have traveled to the outer reaches of our solar system.

698.

The facility's testing capabilities have also been applied to Earth observation satellites, enabling scientists to evaluate the accuracy and reliability of remote sensing instruments used for monitoring our planet's climate and environment.

699.

The TFSS has a rich history of supporting scientific research and development, playing a crucial role in advancing our understanding of the space environment and improving the reliability and performance of spacecraft and satellite systems.

700.

The Twenty-Five-Foot Space Simulator continues to be a vital asset for NASA and the space industry, providing an essential testing ground for future space missions and technological advancements, ensuring that spacecraft can withstand the rigors of the space environment and operate successfully in space exploration endeavors.

701.

The Galapagos Marine Iguana (Amblyrhynchus cristatus) is the only species of marine lizard in the world and is endemic to the Galapagos Islands.

702.

Marine iguanas have a unique adaptation that allows them to forage for food underwater. They can dive up to 30 feet (9 meters) and remain submerged for up to an hour.

703.

They primarily feed on marine algae, which gives them a distinctive green coloration. The algae-rich diet contributes to their nickname, "the only seafaring lizard."

704.

Galapagos Marine Iguanas are known for their unique appearance, characterized by a flattened body, a blunt snout, and a crest of spines along their back.

705.

They have powerful jaws and sharp teeth adapted for grazing on algae-covered rocks along the shoreline.

706.

Marine iguanas are excellent swimmers, using their long, flattened tails to propel themselves through the water.

707.

Their dark coloration helps them absorb heat quickly after they emerge from the water, as they are ectothermic (cold-blooded) and rely on external heat sources to regulate their body temperature.

708.

Marine iguanas exhibit sexual dimorphism, with males growing larger than females. Males can reach lengths of up to 4.9 feet (1.5 meters), while females are typically around 3.6 feet (1.1 meters) long.

709.

During the breeding season, males develop vivid colors on their skin, including bright reds and greens, to attract females.

710.

Galapagos Marine Iguanas are highly territorial and often engage in aggressive behaviors, including head-bobbing and biting, to establish dominance.

711.

Marine iguanas have a unique nasal gland that enables them to expel excess salt from their bodies. They frequently sneeze out saltwater after feeding, earning them the nickname "sneezing iguanas."

712.

The marine iguanas' ability to excrete excess salt through their nasal gland allows them to consume seawater and extract moisture from their food source, helping them survive in the arid conditions of the Galapagos Islands.

713.

Galapagos Marine Iguanas have a lifespan of around 5 to 20 years in the wild, depending on various factors such as predation, food availability, and environmental conditions.

714.

The population size of marine iguanas is closely linked to the availability of their primary food source, marine algae. Changes in algae abundance can affect their population dynamics.

715.

Marine iguanas are considered a vulnerable species due to their restricted habitat range and susceptibility to climate change and introduced predators.

716.

They have a limited distribution within the Galapagos Islands and are found mainly on the rocky shores of Fernandina, Isabela, Santa Cruz, and some smaller islands.

717.

Marine iguanas are important ecological contributors in the Galapagos ecosystem. Their feeding habits help maintain the delicate balance of algae growth, preventing overgrowth that could harm other species.

718.

Marine iguanas have a fascinating evolutionary history. It is believed that they descended from land-dwelling iguanas that arrived in the Galapagos millions of years ago and eventually adapted to a marine lifestyle.

719.

Galapagos Marine Iguanas face natural threats such as predation by birds, including Galapagos hawks and herons, as well as sharks and snakes that prey on young iguanas.

720.

Introduced predators, such as feral cats and rats, pose a significant threat to marine iguanas, particularly during nesting seasons when they can prey on eggs and young hatchlings.

721.

The Galapagos Marine Iguana was once heavily hunted for its meat and oil, which led to significant population declines. Today, hunting of marine iguanas is strictly prohibited.

722.

Marine iguanas have a unique mating system called "leking." Males establish territories on rocky shores, known as leks, and attract females by displaying their colorful skin and engaging in territorial behaviors.

723.

Female marine iguanas lay their eggs in burrows or crevices in the sand or volcanic rocks. The eggs incubate for about three months before hatching.

724.

Galapagos Marine Iguanas practice communal nesting, with multiple females laying their eggs in the same area. This behavior provides protection against predators and helps maintain the temperature and humidity required for successful incubation.

725.

Hatchling marine iguanas face various challenges, including predation by birds and other predators. Only a small percentage of hatchlings survive to reach adulthood.

726.

Marine iguanas have a unique ability to shrink in size during periods of food scarcity. This process, known as "island dwarfism," allows them to survive when food resources are limited.

727.

Galapagos Marine Iguanas are an important tourist attraction in the Galapagos Islands. Visitors have the opportunity to observe and learn about their unique adaptations and behavior.

728.

The presence of marine iguanas is an indicator of the health of the marine ecosystem in the Galapagos. Changes in their population size and behavior can provide insights into the overall ecological balance of the islands.

729.

Marine iguanas have been the subject of scientific research and study for decades, contributing to our understanding of evolution, adaptation, and the interplay between terrestrial and marine ecosystems.

730.

The unique adaptations of marine iguanas, particularly their ability to forage underwater, have inspired researchers studying bio-inspired robotics and underwater locomotion.

731.

Marine iguanas are one of the many fascinating species that contributed to Charles Darwin's theory of evolution. His observations of the diverse wildlife in the Galapagos Islands, including the marine iguanas, played a significant role in shaping his ideas.

732.

Galapagos Marine Iguanas are protected by various conservation efforts, including the establishment of marine protected areas and ongoing monitoring of their populations and habitat.

733.

Climate change poses a significant threat to the survival of marine iguanas. Rising sea temperatures and changes in ocean currents can impact their food availability, leading to population declines.

734.

Efforts are underway to educate local communities and visitors about the importance of conservation and responsible tourism practices to protect marine iguanas and their fragile ecosystem.

735.

The Galapagos Marine Iguana is a flagship species for the Galapagos Islands, representing the unique biodiversity and evolutionary processes that occur in this renowned archipelago.

736.

Galapagos Marine Iguanas have distinct populations on different islands, and ongoing genetic research helps scientists understand the genetic diversity and connectivity between these populations.

737.

Conservation organizations, such as the Galapagos Conservancy and the Charles Darwin Foundation, work collaboratively to monitor and conserve marine iguanas and their habitats.

738.

The Galapagos Marine Iguana has become an icon of the Galapagos Islands and is featured in various forms of art, literature, and media that promote awareness and appreciation for the islands' biodiversity.

739.

Galapagos Marine Iguanas have played a crucial role in shaping the unique ecology of the Galapagos Islands, influencing the evolution of other species through their interactions and behaviors.

740.

Research on marine iguanas has contributed to our understanding of physiological adaptations, such as their ability to tolerate high levels of salt in their bodies and their efficient extraction of nutrients from algae.

741.

Marine iguanas play a significant role in nutrient cycling in the Galapagos ecosystem. The algae they consume contain important nutrients that are released back into the environment through their waste, benefiting other organisms.

742.

The distinctive coloration of marine iguanas, with their shades of black, gray, and green, serves as camouflage, helping them blend in with the rocky volcanic terrain and providing protection from predators.

743.

The Galapagos Marine Iguana is a flagship species for conservation efforts in the Galapagos Islands, drawing attention to the unique challenges faced by endemic species and the need for their protection.

744.

The study of marine iguanas has provided valuable insights into the impacts of El Niño events on their population dynamics and foraging behavior, as these events can cause fluctuations in sea temperatures and food availability.

745.

The Galapagos Marine Iguana has evolved unique cranial adaptations to facilitate their feeding on marine algae, including specialized teeth and jaws that allow them to scrape algae off rocks.

746.

The ecological role of marine iguanas as herbivores helps maintain the balance of the Galapagos Islands' coastal ecosystems by controlling algal growth and promoting the survival of other organisms.

747.

Marine iguanas are known to undergo physiological changes during the breeding season, including an increase in size and the development of breeding colors and crests to attract mates.

748.

The study of marine iguanas has provided valuable insights into the effects of human disturbances, such as tourism and pollution, on their behavior, reproduction, and overall population health.

749.

Marine iguanas have been observed engaging in a behavior known as "sneaker male" strategy, where smaller males mimic females to avoid confrontation with dominant males and gain access to mating opportunities.

750.

The Galapagos Marine Iguana exemplifies the remarkable adaptability of organisms to extreme environments and serves as a

symbol of the Galapagos Islands' unique biodiversity and
conservation importance.

751.

The Galapagos Masked Booby Bird (Sula dactylatra) is a large
seabird species endemic to the Galapagos Islands.

752.

It is known for its distinct appearance, with a black body, white
head, and a yellowish or bluish beak.

753.

The masked booby gets its name from the dark mask-like feathers
around its eyes.

754.

It is one of the largest species of boobies, with adults reaching
lengths of about 32 inches (81 cm) and wingspans of up to 5.9 feet
(1.8 meters).

755.

The masked booby is a skilled diver and can plunge into the water
from heights of up to 100 feet (30 meters) to catch fish.

756.

These birds are known for their graceful flight and can cover long
distances while searching for food.

757.

The Galapagos Islands are home to one of the largest populations of
masked boobies in the world.

758.

The masked booby is a colonial nester, often nesting in large colonies on rocky cliffs or sandy beaches.

759.

Mating pairs of masked boobies form long-term partnerships and exhibit strong pair bonds.

760.

During the courtship display, male masked boobies perform elaborate dances and present nesting materials to females to attract their attention.

761.

The female masked booby typically lays one to three eggs in a simple nest constructed from twigs and vegetation.

762.

Both parents take turns incubating the eggs, with incubation periods lasting around 45 days.

763.

The chicks are initially covered in white down feathers and rely on their parents for food and protection.

764.

Young masked booby chicks have a distinctive appearance with a brownish plumage and white faces.

765.

The Galapagos Masked Booby is a skilled fisherman, feeding mainly on small fish, squid, and other marine organisms.

766.

They often dive headfirst into the water to catch their prey, using their sharp beak to snatch fish near the surface.

767.

The masked booby is known to engage in cooperative hunting, where multiple individuals work together to drive fish to the surface, making it easier to catch them.

768.

These seabirds have a unique adaptation that enables them to consume saltwater without harming themselves. They have specialized glands located above their eyes that filter out excess salt from their bloodstream.

769.

The masked booby has excellent eyesight, which helps them spot prey from great distances while flying above the ocean.

770.

Galapagos Masked Boobies are highly territorial during the breeding season and fiercely defend their nesting sites from intruders.

771.

The abundance of fish in the Galapagos marine ecosystem is a crucial factor in determining the success of masked booby breeding seasons.

772.

In years when food is scarce, masked boobies may delay breeding or lay fewer eggs to ensure the survival of their offspring.

773.

These seabirds are known for their distinctive vocalizations, including loud honking and grunting sounds made during courtship and territorial disputes.

774.

The masked booby has few natural predators in the Galapagos Islands, with their large size and aggressive behavior deterring most potential threats.

775.

Introduced predators, such as rats and cats, pose a significant risk to masked booby populations, particularly to their eggs and chicks.

776.

The Galapagos Masked Booby has been classified as a species of least concern by the International Union for Conservation of Nature (IUCN) due to its relatively stable population and widespread distribution.

777.

Climate change poses a potential threat to the masked booby's habitat and food availability, as changes in ocean currents and temperature can affect fish populations.

778.

The Galapagos Islands provide important breeding grounds for the masked booby, with protected areas and conservation efforts helping to maintain their population and nesting habitats.

779.

The health of the masked booby population serves as an indicator of the overall health of the Galapagos marine ecosystem.

780.

Researchers study the feeding behaviors and movements of masked boobies to gain insights into the health and dynamics of the Galapagos marine food web.

781.

The Galapagos Masked Booby is an iconic species of the Galapagos Islands and is often featured in nature documentaries and ecotourism activities.

782.

The presence of masked boobies in the Galapagos Islands has historical significance, as Charles Darwin observed and studied these birds during his voyage on the HMS Beagle, contributing to his theory of evolution.

783.

The Galapagos Masked Booby is known to engage in "sky-pointing" behavior, where they raise their bills and gaze skyward as a form of communication or territorial display.

784.

The feathers of the masked booby are highly specialized to resist the corrosive effects of saltwater, protecting the birds' bodies during their frequent contact with the ocean.

785.

The masked booby has a unique mating system where females are often outnumbered by males, leading to intense competition among males for mating opportunities.

786.

Galapagos Masked Boobies are capable of long-distance migrations, and individuals have been recorded traveling as far as mainland South America.

787.

The masked booby plays a crucial role in the nutrient cycling of the Galapagos marine ecosystem. Their guano (excrement) contributes to the fertility of the islands' soils, benefiting plant growth and supporting other species.

788.

These birds are known for their resilience and adaptability, allowing them to thrive in the challenging conditions of the Galapagos Islands.

789.

The Galapagos Masked Booby is a subject of ongoing research and monitoring to better understand its population dynamics, breeding success, and interactions with other species.

790.

Conservation organizations, such as the Galapagos National Park Directorate, work to protect the nesting sites and habitats of the masked booby and implement measures to mitigate the impact of introduced predators.

791.

Visitors to the Galapagos Islands have the opportunity to observe masked boobies during guided tours and wildlife excursions, providing valuable educational experiences and raising awareness about the importance of seabird conservation.

792.

The breeding success of the masked booby is closely tied to the health of the surrounding marine environment, making their conservation a priority for maintaining the ecological balance of the Galapagos Islands.

793.

The Galapagos Masked Booby is known for its agility in flight, often performing aerial acrobatics and displaying intricate flight patterns.

794.

The Galapagos Islands provide a protected and relatively undisturbed environment for the masked booby, allowing researchers to study their behavior, population dynamics, and ecological interactions in detail.

795.

The Galapagos Masked Booby is a flagship species for conservation efforts in the Galapagos Islands, symbolizing the unique biodiversity and ecological significance of this iconic archipelago.

796.

The marine environment surrounding the Galapagos Islands serves as a vital feeding ground for the masked booby, offering abundant food resources that support their breeding success and overall population health.

797.

The Galapagos Masked Booby has coexisted with other unique bird species in the Galapagos Islands for thousands of years, resulting in distinct adaptations and ecological interactions.

798.

The Galapagos Masked Booby is part of a larger ecosystem of seabirds in the Galapagos, including other booby species such as the Blue-footed Booby and the Red-footed Booby.

799.

The masked booby is known for its strong sense of homing, returning to the same nesting site year after year, even after extensive foraging trips at sea.

800.

The Galapagos Masked Booby serves as a symbol of the resilience and beauty of the Galapagos Islands' wildlife and underscores the importance of protecting these unique and fragile ecosystems for future generations.

801.

General Mills is a multinational food company headquartered in Minneapolis, Minnesota, United States.

802.

The company was originally founded on June 20, 1856, as the Minneapolis Milling Company by Robert Smith, with the goal of producing flour to meet the growing demand in the region.

803.

In 1866, Cadwallader C. Washburn purchased the Minneapolis Milling Company and renamed it Washburn Crosby Company.

804.

The company's flagship product, Gold Medal Flour, was introduced in 1880 and quickly gained a reputation for its high quality.

805.

The Washburn Crosby Company became a major player in the flour milling industry and began expanding its product portfolio to include cereals and other food products.

806.

In 1921, the company merged with 26 other mills to form the General Mills Corporation, taking its name from the popular brand of flour it produced.

807.

During World War II, General Mills played a crucial role in supplying the U.S. military with nutritious and easy-to-prepare meals for soldiers.

808.

In the 1950s, General Mills introduced several iconic cereal brands, including Cheerios, Trix, and Lucky Charms, which became household names and remain popular today.

809.

The company pioneered the use of radio and television advertising to promote its products, launching successful campaigns that helped establish its brands in the minds of consumers.

810.

General Mills expanded its operations internationally in the 1960s, establishing subsidiaries and acquiring food companies in Canada, Europe, and Australia.

811.

In 1961, General Mills introduced the first frozen pizza, known as Totino's Pizza, which revolutionized the convenience food industry.

812.

The company continued to diversify its product offerings, acquiring various food brands, including Betty Crocker, Pillsbury, and Yoplait, among others.

813.

General Mills became a leader in the packaged foods industry, offering a wide range of products, including baking mixes, snacks, yogurt, cereal bars, and frozen meals.

814.

In 1970, General Mills acquired the rights to market and distribute Häagen-Dazs ice cream in the United States, helping to popularize the brand and expand its presence globally.

815.

In the 1980s, General Mills made a strategic move to focus on the health and wellness segment, introducing low-fat and high-fiber products to meet changing consumer preferences.

816.

The company faced challenges in the 1990s as health-conscious consumers shifted away from traditional processed foods, leading General Mills to invest in healthier alternatives and expand its organic and natural product offerings.

817.

General Mills established the General Mills Foundation in 1954, which has since contributed millions of dollars in grants to support education, hunger relief, and community development programs.

818.

General Mills has a strong commitment to sustainability and has implemented various initiatives to reduce its environmental footprint, such as improving energy efficiency, reducing greenhouse gas emissions, and promoting sustainable sourcing practices.

819.

The company has been recognized for its efforts in promoting diversity and inclusion, earning accolades for its diverse workforce, inclusive policies, and support for underrepresented communities.

820.

General Mills has been involved in various philanthropic partnerships and initiatives to address hunger and food insecurity, both locally and globally.

821.

The company has a long history of supporting agricultural research and development, working closely with farmers and suppliers to promote sustainable farming practices and ensure the quality and safety of its products.

822.

General Mills has been a leader in food innovation, continuously introducing new products and adapting to changing consumer preferences. Some notable innovations include gluten-free Cheerios and Nature Valley protein bars.

823.

The company has faced criticism and legal challenges over the years, including lawsuits related to health claims, labeling practices, and allegations of deceptive marketing.

824.

General Mills has a strong commitment to food safety and quality control, maintaining rigorous standards and implementing comprehensive testing procedures to ensure the safety of its products.

825.

General Mills has received numerous awards and recognition for its corporate responsibility efforts, including being named one of the World's Most Ethical Companies by Ethisphere Institute.

826.

The company has a significant presence in the breakfast cereal market, holding a strong market share with popular brands like Cheerios, Wheaties, and Cocoa Puffs.

827.

General Mills has expanded its product portfolio to cater to evolving consumer preferences, introducing organic and natural brands such as Annie's, Cascadian Farm, and LÄRABAR.

828.

The company has embraced digital transformation and e-commerce, investing in online platforms and digital marketing strategies to reach consumers directly and adapt to the changing retail landscape.

829.

General Mills has a history of engaging in strategic partnerships and collaborations, working with other food companies, nonprofit organizations, and research institutions to drive innovation and address industry challenges.

830.

General Mills has been recognized for its efforts in reducing food waste, implementing initiatives to minimize waste throughout its supply chain and partnering with organizations to rescue surplus food.

831.

The company has a strong focus on consumer insights and research, conducting market studies and surveys to understand consumer preferences and develop products that meet their needs.

832.

General Mills has a strong commitment to promoting nutrition education and awareness, providing resources and programs to help consumers make informed choices about their diet and lifestyle.

833.

The company has made efforts to reformulate its products to reduce sugar, sodium, and artificial ingredients, responding to concerns about the nutritional content of processed foods.

834.

General Mills is listed on the New York Stock Exchange under the ticker symbol GIS and is included in the S&P 500 index.

835.

The company's iconic Betty Crocker brand, known for its baking mixes and recipes, has become a household name synonymous with home baking and cooking.

836.

General Mills has a robust research and development division, employing scientists, food technologists, and culinary experts to drive innovation and develop new products.

837.

General Mills has a global workforce of thousands of employees, working across various functions, including manufacturing, marketing, research, finance, and supply chain management.

838.

The company operates manufacturing facilities and distribution centers in multiple countries, ensuring efficient production and timely delivery of its products to consumers worldwide.

839.

General Mills has embraced digital marketing and social media platforms, leveraging these channels to engage with consumers, build brand loyalty, and gather feedback.

840.

The company has a history of adapting its products to meet the cultural preferences and dietary needs of different regions, tailoring flavors, ingredients, and packaging to local markets.

841.

General Mills has faced challenges in recent years related to changing consumer preferences and increased competition from smaller, niche food companies that focus on natural and organic products.

842.

The company has responded to these challenges by acquiring smaller, innovative brands that align with evolving consumer trends, such as the acquisition of Annie's, a leading organic and natural food brand.

843.

General Mills has made significant investments in digital capabilities and data analytics, leveraging technology to better understand consumer behavior and optimize marketing strategies.

844.

The company has a strong commitment to corporate governance and ethical business practices, maintaining a Code of Conduct that guides employees in their professional conduct and decision-making.

845.

General Mills has been recognized for its workplace culture and employee benefits, receiving awards for its commitment to diversity, employee engagement, and work-life balance.

846.

The company actively engages with local communities through philanthropic initiatives, employee volunteer programs, and partnerships with nonprofit organizations.

847.

General Mills has a history of successfully navigating changing consumer preferences and market dynamics, adapting its product portfolio to remain relevant and competitive.

848.

The company has a robust supply chain management system, ensuring the efficient sourcing of raw materials, manufacturing, and distribution of its products to meet consumer demand.

849.

General Mills has a strong track record of financial performance, delivering consistent revenue growth and shareholder value over the years.

850.

As a prominent player in the food industry, General Mills continues to evolve and innovate, working towards its mission of "making food people love" while embracing sustainability, health, and consumer-centricity.

851.

Levi Strauss & Co. is a globally renowned clothing company, best known for its iconic denim jeans.

852.

The company was founded in 1853 in San Francisco, California, by Levi Strauss, a German-American businessman.

853.

Levi Strauss originally immigrated to the United States from Bavaria, Germany, during the California Gold Rush.

854.

Initially, Levi Strauss operated a dry goods wholesale business, selling a variety of goods including clothing, fabric, and other supplies.

855.

Levi Strauss partnered with Jacob Davis, a tailor from Nevada, to create a durable work pant made of denim fabric with copper rivets for reinforcement.

856.

On May 20, 1873, the two partners received a patent for their innovation, which marked the birth of the classic blue jeans.

857.

The first jeans produced by Levi Strauss & Co. were known as the "XX" and featured the iconic red tab and leather patch at the back.

858.

Levi Strauss & Co. played a significant role in outfitting workers during the American Westward Expansion, providing durable clothing suitable for miners, cowboys, and laborers.

859.

The company's blue jeans gained popularity for their durability and quality, becoming the garment of choice for hardworking individuals across America.

860.

During World War II, Levi Strauss & Co. switched production to support the war effort, making uniforms and other military garments for the U.S. armed forces.

861.

Levi Strauss & Co. expanded its international presence in the 1960s, opening factories and stores in various countries around the world.

862.

The Levi's brand gained cultural significance during the countercultural movements of the 1960s and 1970s, becoming a symbol of rebellion and youthful expression.

863.

Levi's jeans were featured prominently in popular culture, including films, music, and fashion, further cementing their iconic status.

864.

The Levi's 501 model, introduced in the late 19th century, remains one of the company's most enduring and popular jean styles.

865.

In the 1980s, Levi Strauss & Co. faced competition from other denim brands and experienced a decline in sales. However, the company successfully repositioned itself and regained market share in subsequent years.

866.

Levi Strauss & Co. has been a pioneer in corporate social responsibility, implementing various initiatives to promote sustainable practices, worker well-being, and community engagement.

867.

The company has been committed to water conservation and reducing its environmental impact, implementing innovative technologies to minimize water usage in denim production.

868.

Levi Strauss & Co. launched the "Levi's Water<Less" initiative, which significantly reduces the water consumption in the finishing process of jeans.

869.

Levi Strauss & Co. has been an advocate for LGBTQ+ rights, with a long-standing commitment to inclusivity and equality. The company was one of the first to offer same-sex partner benefits to employees.

870.

The iconic Levi's logo, known as the "batwing," features the company name and a pair of jeans, symbolizing the heritage and quality associated with the brand.

871.

Levi Strauss & Co. has expanded its product offerings beyond jeans, including a wide range of clothing and accessories, such as shirts, jackets, dresses, and footwear.

872.

The company has collaborated with various fashion designers, artists, and brands to create limited-edition collections and unique product lines.

873.

Levi Strauss & Co. has faced criticism and controversy over labor practices in some of its global supply chains, leading the company to strengthen its commitment to ethical sourcing and fair labor standards.

874.

In 2019, Levi Strauss & Co. became a publicly traded company once again, with its shares listed on the New York Stock Exchange under the ticker symbol LEVI.

875.

The Levi Strauss Foundation, established in 1952, supports numerous philanthropic initiatives globally, focusing on education, social justice, and community development.

876.

Levi Strauss & Co. has a rich archival collection that preserves the history and heritage of the company, including vintage garments, photographs, and advertising materials.

877.

The Levi Strauss & Co. headquarters, known as the Levi's Plaza, is located in San Francisco and serves as a hub for the company's operations and design.

878.

The company has a strong commitment to innovation, constantly exploring new materials, technologies, and design approaches to meet the evolving needs and preferences of consumers.

879.

Levi Strauss & Co. has been recognized for its efforts in reducing its carbon footprint and implementing sustainable practices, receiving certifications such as LEED (Leadership in Energy and Environmental Design) for its eco-friendly buildings.

880.

The Levi Strauss Archives, located in San Francisco, houses an extensive collection of historical artifacts and documents that provide insights into the company's evolution and impact on popular culture.

881.

The Levi Strauss & Co. brand has been featured in museum exhibitions worldwide, highlighting the cultural significance and enduring legacy of the company.

882.

Levi Strauss & Co. has established partnerships with nonprofit organizations to promote education, job training, and empowerment in underserved communities.

883.

The company has embraced e-commerce and digital marketing, offering online shopping options and engaging with consumers through social media and other digital platforms.

884.

Levi's jeans have been worn by numerous celebrities, musicians, and cultural icons, further solidifying the brand's association with style and authenticity.

885.

Levi Strauss & Co. has a history of supporting local arts and culture initiatives, sponsoring events, exhibitions, and festivals that celebrate creativity and expression.

886.

The company has received numerous awards and accolades for its corporate social responsibility efforts, including recognition as one of the World's Most Ethical Companies by Ethisphere Institute.

887.

Levi's jeans have evolved in style and design over the years, reflecting changing fashion trends while maintaining the core elements that make them timeless and iconic.

888.

Levi Strauss & Co. has a strong commitment to diversity and inclusion, both within its workforce and in its marketing campaigns, representing people of various backgrounds and body types.

889.

The Levi Strauss Foundation supports organizations and initiatives dedicated to advancing LGBTQ+ equality, immigrant rights, and addressing economic disparities.

890.

The Levi's brand has remained relevant and resonant across generations, appealing to consumers of different ages and cultural backgrounds.

891.

The company has embraced digital transformation, utilizing data analytics and technology to gain insights into consumer preferences, improve supply chain efficiency, and enhance the overall customer experience.

892.

Levi Strauss & Co. has a long history of advocating for positive change in the fashion industry, collaborating with other companies and industry organizations to promote sustainable practices and ethical standards.

893.

The Levi Strauss & Co. brand is recognized globally and has a presence in over 110 countries, with stores, distribution centers, and manufacturing facilities worldwide.

894.

The company has a robust employee volunteer program, encouraging its staff to engage in community service and contribute to social and environmental initiatives.

895.

Levi Strauss & Co. has actively promoted worker well-being and safety, implementing programs and initiatives to ensure the health and welfare of its employees and suppliers.

896.

The company has been recognized for its commitment to gender equality and women's empowerment, with initiatives focused on advancing women's leadership and supporting women-owned businesses.

897.

Levi Strauss & Co. has a strong commitment to transparency and corporate governance, regularly publishing sustainability reports and disclosing its environmental and social impact.

898.

The Levi's brand has become synonymous with American culture, representing a spirit of independence, authenticity, and individuality.

899.

The company's commitment to philanthropy and social responsibility extends to disaster relief efforts, with Levi Strauss & Co.supporting communities affected by natural disasters through financial contributions and employee volunteerism.

900.

Levi Strauss & Co. continues to evolve and innovate, staying true to its heritage while adapting to changing consumer preferences and global trends in the fashion industry.

901.

The Unitary Plan Wind Tunnel (UPWT) is a world-class facility used for aerodynamic testing of various vehicles, structures, and objects.

902.

It was constructed by NASA's Langley Research Center in Hampton, Virginia, United States.

903.

The UPWT was designed to provide precise and controlled wind flow conditions, allowing engineers and scientists to study the aerodynamic behavior of different objects.

904.

The wind tunnel features a closed-loop system, where air is recirculated continuously to create consistent and repeatable testing conditions.

905.

The UPWT is capable of generating wind speeds up to Mach 0.3, which is approximately one-third of the speed of sound.

906.

The wind tunnel is equipped with a powerful fan system that can generate wind speeds of up to 200 miles per hour (322 kilometers per hour).

907.

The facility has a test section with dimensions of approximately 80 feet (24 meters) long, 16 feet (4.9 meters) wide, and 16 feet (4.9 meters) tall.

908.

The UPWT can accommodate large-scale models, including aircraft, spacecraft, vehicles, and even architectural structures.

909.

It is often used to test and improve the aerodynamic performance of aircraft, including wings, fuselages, and other components.

910.

The wind tunnel allows engineers to assess the lift, drag, and stability characteristics of different vehicles under various wind conditions.

911.

The UPWT is used in the development and design of various types of vehicles, including airplanes, helicopters, cars, trains, and even high-speed boats.

912.

Wind tunnel testing at the UPWT helps optimize vehicle performance, fuel efficiency, and safety.

913.

The facility is equipped with advanced instrumentation and measurement systems to gather accurate data on airflow patterns, pressure distribution, and other aerodynamic parameters.

914.

Engineers use the wind tunnel to study and improve the efficiency of airfoils, which are crucial for generating lift in aircraft wings.

915.

The UPWT enables researchers to investigate the effects of wind on buildings, bridges, and other structures, ensuring their stability and safety under different wind loads.

916.

Wind tunnel testing helps engineers evaluate and optimize the performance of wind turbines, enhancing their energy conversion efficiency.

917.

The UPWT has contributed to advancements in aviation, aerospace, and transportation industries by providing critical aerodynamic data for the design of more efficient and safer vehicles.

918.

The wind tunnel allows for testing in both subsonic and transonic regimes, covering a wide range of aerodynamic conditions.

919.

Researchers can simulate various flight scenarios, such as takeoff, landing, cruising, and maneuvering, to understand the aerodynamic characteristics of different vehicles at different stages of flight.

920.

The UPWT has played a significant role in the development of supersonic and hypersonic flight technologies, including the study of shock waves and boundary layer behavior.

921.

The facility is used to validate and refine computational fluid dynamics (CFD) models, which simulate airflow around objects, ensuring the accuracy of numerical simulations.

922.

Wind tunnel testing at the UPWT is crucial for verifying and fine-tuning computer models used in the design and optimization of vehicles and structures.

923.

The UPWT has been in operation for several decades, continuously contributing to the advancement of aerodynamics and engineering knowledge.

924.

The wind tunnel is operated by a team of skilled engineers, technicians, and scientists who oversee the testing process and ensure the accuracy of the results.

925.

The UPWT is often used by NASA and other government agencies for research and development purposes.

926.

The facility is also available for use by private companies, research institutions, and universities for their aerodynamic testing needs.

927.

Wind tunnel testing at the UPWT helps reduce the risks associated with vehicle development, ensuring that vehicles perform as expected in real-world conditions.

928.

The wind tunnel's large test section allows for the testing of full-scale or scaled-down models, depending on the research requirements.

929.

The UPWT provides a controlled environment for testing, eliminating external factors such as turbulence and other weather conditions that could affect results.

930.

The wind tunnel is equipped with a sophisticated data acquisition system that captures and analyzes large amounts of aerodynamic data during testing.

931.

The UPWT has been used for numerous research projects related to aviation safety, aircraft design optimization, and vehicle efficiency improvements.

932.

The facility has contributed to advancements in noise reduction technologies by studying the aerodynamic sources of noise and developing quieter vehicle designs.

933.

Wind tunnel testing at the UPWT allows researchers to study the effects of different airflow conditions on vehicle stability, control, and handling characteristics.

934.

The facility has been used to investigate the aerodynamic forces and loads experienced by vehicles in extreme weather conditions, such as strong winds and gusts.

935.

The UPWT has played a role in the development of unmanned aerial vehicles (UAVs) by testing their aerodynamic performance and stability.

936.

Wind tunnel testing at the UPWT helps engineers optimize the placement and design of control surfaces, such as ailerons, elevators, and rudders, to ensure precise and responsive vehicle control.

937.

The wind tunnel provides a controlled environment for the testing of unconventional vehicle designs, such as flying cars or futuristic aircraft concepts.

938.

The UPWT has been used for research on the effects of ice accumulation on aircraft surfaces, helping to develop anti-icing and de-icing technologies.

939.

Wind tunnel testing at the facility enables engineers to study the effects of airflow on engine performance and efficiency, contributing to advancements in propulsion systems.

940.

The UPWT has contributed to the development of advanced aerodynamic concepts, such as laminar flow control, which reduces drag and improves fuel efficiency.

941.

The wind tunnel has been used to study the effects of aerodynamic forces on aircraft structures, helping to enhance their durability and safety.

942.

Wind tunnel testing at the UPWT has been used to investigate the aerodynamic characteristics of unconventional vehicles, such as high-speed trains and hyperloop systems.

943.

The facility has been instrumental in the development of technologies for mitigating aerodynamic noise, improving the comfort of passengers and reducing noise pollution.

944.

The UPWT has been used for research on the effects of atmospheric conditions, such as turbulence and wind gusts, on vehicle stability and control.

945.

Wind tunnel testing at the facility enables researchers to study the flow behavior around complex geometries, such as aircraft wings with intricate shapes or unconventional vehicle designs.

946.

The UPWT has contributed to the development of wind engineering and wind load standards, ensuring the safety and stability of buildings and structures in windy environments.

947.

Wind tunnel testing at the facility allows engineers to investigate the effects of wind on vehicle aerodynamics during different flight phases, such as climb, cruise, and descent.

948.

The UPWT has contributed to advancements in parachute design and optimization, ensuring safe and effective parachutes for various applications.

949.

Wind tunnel testing at the facility has been used to study the effects of wind on outdoor sports activities, such as cycling, skiing, and racing, improving athlete performance and safety.

950.

The UPWT continues to play a vital role in aerodynamic research and development, providing essential data and insights for the design and optimization of vehicles and structures in various industries.

951.

Walker Pass is a mountain pass located in the southern Sierra Nevada mountain range in California, United States.

952.

The pass is situated at an elevation of 5,246 feet (1,599 meters) above sea level.

953.

Walker Pass is named after Joseph R. Walker, an American explorer and mountain man who discovered the route in 1834.

954.

The pass serves as a significant transportation route, connecting the eastern and western regions of California.

955.

It is located on State Route 178, which is a popular scenic drive known as the Walker Pass Scenic Byway.

956.

The pass offers breathtaking views of the surrounding mountains, including the dramatic peaks of the southern Sierra Nevada range.

957.

Walker Pass is known for its challenging terrain and steep grades, making it a popular destination for hikers and cyclists seeking a thrilling outdoor adventure.

958.

The area around Walker Pass is rich in natural beauty and wildlife, with opportunities for birdwatching, wildflower spotting, and photography.

959.

The pass is a historical route that was once used by Native American tribes for trade and travel.

960.

During the California Gold Rush of the mid-19th century, Walker Pass served as a crucial route for miners and pioneers heading to the goldfields.

961.

The pass was also utilized by early settlers and traders during the westward expansion of the United States.

962.

Walker Pass played a role in the development of the Owens Valley, as it provided a gateway for settlers to access the fertile lands of the valley.

963.

The pass has a rich Native American history, with evidence of habitation and cultural sites in the surrounding area.

964.

Walker Pass is situated within the Inyo National Forest, offering visitors opportunities for camping, hiking, and exploring the natural surroundings.

965.

The pass is part of the Pacific Crest Trail, a long-distance hiking trail that stretches from Mexico to Canada.

966.

Hikers and backpackers often pass through Walker Pass as they journey along the Pacific Crest Trail, taking advantage of its amenities and resupply options.

967.

Walker Pass is known for its extreme weather conditions, with hot summers and cold winters. Travelers are advised to be prepared for sudden changes in weather and temperature.

968.

The pass is a popular spot for stargazing due to its remote location and minimal light pollution.

969.

Walker Pass has been featured in various movies and television shows, serving as a backdrop for desert and mountain scenes.

970.

The pass is home to a diverse range of plant species, including Joshua trees, pinyon pines, and various wildflowers.

971.

Wildlife in the area includes mule deer, coyotes, rabbits, and a variety of bird species.

972.

Walker Pass offers opportunities for rock climbing and bouldering, with several notable climbing routes in the surrounding mountains.

973.

The pass provides access to the Domeland Wilderness, a protected wilderness area known for its rugged terrain and stunning landscapes.

974.

The Walker Basin Conservancy, a nonprofit organization, is actively involved in the conservation and restoration of the ecological health of the Walker Basin area.

975.

The pass has historical markers and interpretive signs that provide information about its significance and history.

976.

The nearby town of Ridgecrest, located east of Walker Pass, serves as a gateway to outdoor recreational activities in the region.

977.

Walker Pass is a favorite destination for motorcycle enthusiasts, who enjoy the scenic ride and challenging road conditions.

978.

The area around the pass is known for its geological formations, including exposed rock layers and unique geological features.

979.

Walker Pass is situated along the Great Basin Divide, which separates water flowing into the Pacific Ocean from water flowing into the Great Basin.

980.

The pass is located within Kern County, California, and is approximately 50 miles (80 kilometers) east of Bakersfield.

981.

Walker Pass is part of the historical Old Spanish Trail, a trade route that connected Santa Fe, New Mexico, with Los Angeles, California, during the 19th century.

982.

The pass has been used for meteorological research, providing valuable data on wind patterns and atmospheric conditions.

983.

Walker Pass is a popular destination for fall foliage viewing, as the surrounding mountains are adorned with vibrant colors during the autumn season.

984.

The pass has rest areas and picnic spots, providing travelers with a chance to take a break and enjoy the scenic surroundings.

985.

Walker Pass is known for its strong winds, especially during the winter months, which can create challenging driving conditions.

986.

The pass has been a site for archaeological investigations, uncovering artifacts and evidence of past human activities in the region.

987.

Walker Pass is named as one of the key historical landmarks on the California Historical Landmark registry.

988.

The pass provides access to the South Fork Kern River, which is popular for fishing and camping.

989.

The area around Walker Pass is known for its unique geological formations, including granite outcroppings and volcanic rocks.

990.

The pass has been traversed by famous explorers and pioneers, including John C. Frémont and the infamous Death Valley 49ers.

991.

The surrounding mountains offer opportunities for backcountry skiing and snowboarding during the winter months.

992.

Walker Pass is located near the southern entrance of the Sequoia National Forest, offering visitors access to the stunning giant sequoia groves.

993.

The pass is a designated California Scenic Highway, highlighting its natural beauty and historical significance.

994.

Walker Pass has been used for military training exercises due to its challenging terrain and remote location.

995.

The area around the pass is known for its diverse bird population, attracting birdwatchers from around the region.

996.

The pass has been a subject of artistic inspiration, with painters and photographers capturing its scenic beauty.

997.

Walker Pass is situated within the traditional lands of Native American tribes, including the Kawaiisu and Tubatulabal people.

998.

The pass has been featured in literature and novels, serving as a backdrop for stories set in the rugged landscapes of the American West.

999.

Walker Pass offers opportunities for off-road enthusiasts, with nearby trails suitable for off-roading and four-wheel driving.

1000.

The pass continues to be an important transportation route, serving as a link between the eastern and western regions of California, and attracting outdoor enthusiasts, history buffs, and nature lovers alike.

9 798851 421617